Anglicans in Rome

Frederick M. Bliss SM teaches Ecumenical theology at the
Angelicum University in Rome

Anglicans
in
Rome

A History

Frederick M. Bliss SM

CANTERBURY
PRESS
Norwich

in association with the
Friends of the Anglican Centre in Rome

© Frederick Bliss SM 2006

First published in 2006 by the Canterbury Press Norwich
(a publishing imprint of Hymns Ancient & Modern Limited,
a registered charity)
9–17 St Alban's Place, London
NI ONX

www.scm-canterburypress.co.uk

British Library Cataloguing in Publication data

A catalogue record for this book is available
from the British Library

ISBN 1-85311-745-5/978-1-85311-745-9

Typeset by Regent Typesetting, London
Printed and bound in Great Britain by
William Clowes Ltd, Beccles, Suffolk

Contents

Contents

Contents

Foreword

Despite all the mutual rejections, cruelties and recriminations, many of them rooted in the Reformation era, some contacts between Anglicans and Roman Catholics have always continued. But only in the twentieth century, with explorations such as the Malines conversations, did the impetus to seek actively for unity begin to gather momentum. The Second Vatican Council gave this a most welcome new boost, and the process of officially sponsored conversations, which started as a consequence of the council, has allowed significant progress, in both mutual understanding and collaboration. It may seem that the pace has slackened in more recent years, but there is still forward movement that not only involves designated representatives, but is increasingly becoming co-operation and spiritual fellowship in local situations. Those who can remember the glacial divides of the years immediately after 1945 know how different things are today, and how much there is to thank God for in the present situation.

The work of a whole series of Representatives of the Archbishops of Canterbury to the Holy See, and Directors of the Anglican Centre in Rome, has been a significant ingredient in the total search for reconciliation. During my time as Director of the Centre and Archbishop's Representative, I realized that the time had come for a writing-up of the work of many people who had given time and great talent to it, especially since a good number of people are still alive and have personal memories of its origins. They have given a wider picture than documents alone could ever do.

Foreword

I was delighted when Father Frederick Bliss SM said – with his characteristic practical and unassuming kindliness – that he would do the work. Fred is a prominent teacher of Ecumenics at the Angelicum University, an institution which trains men for the Roman Catholic priesthood, many of them for service in English-speaking communities.

I am sure that the results of Fred's clear and readable work will be very interesting to a general readership, and especially to students and seminarians who are seeking a straightforward basic and accurate grasp of a significant aspect of the world-wide search for Christian unity and also of the tried and tested method that can inform the way the search can be conducted in the future.

There is much to thank God for, yet there is still much more to be done.

+Richard Garrard
December 2005

Preface

George Edmund Street's two magnificent churches of All Saints' and St Paul-within-the-Walls testify to the existence of Anglican communities within Rome well before the twentieth century. Nevertheless, it was undoubtedly the historic visit to Rome of Archbishop Geoffrey Fisher in 1960, and the more comprehensive visit of Archbishop Michael Ramsey in 1966, which were ground breaking in re-establishing formal links between our two communions. Fisher's visit was remarkable as being the first meeting between an Archbishop of Canterbury and a Pope since the Reformation. Indeed, the previous visit of an Archbishop of Canterbury to a Pope was that of Archbishop Arundel in 1397. Ramsey's visit was seminal, since it came at the time of the Second Vatican Council and the burgeoning of a new movement towards unity among all the churches, presaged within the Roman Catholic Church by the Decree on Ecumenism *Unitatis Redintegratio* of 1964.

Both the decree itself, and the Council more widely, had an energizing effect within what had already become dubbed the ecumenical century, beginning with the Edinburgh Conference in 1910. The meeting between Pope Paul VI and Archbishop Michael Ramsey was further aided by the Pope's prior knowledge of Anglicanism and of his friendship with a number of Anglican clergy while he had been Cardinal Archbishop of Milan. Out of this encounter emerged the Malta Commission, which eventually led to the establishment of the first Anglican–Roman Catholic International Commission. Alongside this, and of great significance too, was the foundation of the Anglican

Centre in Rome. Founded by Archbishop Ramsey, with the encouragement of the Holy Father and with the assistance of Bishop John Moorman (one of the Anglican observers at the Vatican Council), its existence was ultimately only made possible by the generosity of Principessa Orietta Doria Pamphylj and her family. The continuing generosity and support of this Anglo-Italian Roman Catholic family has led to the Centre's prospering now for some 40 years.

This fortieth anniversary year is an excellent moment not only to take stock of the contribution of the different Anglican communities in Rome, but also to look to the future to see how that contribution may be both fostered and expanded. The Centre has been fortunate in being able to call upon the talents of a varied group of directors and supporters over these years. Two of the directors have been Australian Anglicans and another a Canadian; the other directors have come from the Church of England. The directors have included among their number three bishops, a monk, a cathedral canon and a professor of theology. Directors have given tirelessly to establishing the Centre, consolidating its work and overseeing the complex process of relocation within the Palazzo Doria. It is indeed a happy coincidence to report that the daughter of the first director still lives in Rome. The life of the Centre now is perhaps more lively and influential than ever.

The Centre and the other Anglican communities in Rome have seen vast changes in the relationship between our two communions in the past 50 years. From the four centuries of comparative isolation has followed almost half a century of ecumenical progress. Even the difficulties and hurdles of recent years still see our communions closer to each other than ever might have been imagined before the advent of the Second Vatican Council. The Anglican–Roman Catholic International Commission has pioneered bilateral ecclesial dialogue, and many of its documents now act as touchstones and reference points for ecumenical theologians and ecclesiologists. This book is itself a further contribution to our growing together, as was the Vatican Museum Exhibition on Anglicanism of 2003 and the associated colloquium. From the outset, all engaged in ecumenical dialogue have been clear that theological agreement is but one part of a far larger whole. That wider canvas includes a growing together and deeper mutual knowledge of each other's communities. Part of that must be an understanding of our histories. This history of Anglicans in Rome will play a unique part in all this, remembering the importance of the city of Rome in the early development of our faith, and its present significance for Roman Catholicism, the single largest communion within the wider Christian family. It is a marvellous and positive irony to be able to thank Father Fred Bliss, a Roman Catholic religious, for offering to write this history on behalf of Anglicans in Rome.

+Stephen Platten
Epiphany 2006

Introduction

As I sifted through hundreds of pages in the archives of the Rome Anglican Centre on Anglican–Catholic relations, I recalled Kenneth Clark's celebrated series of the late 1960s, *Civilisation*. In one episode he referred to the cultural consolidation that identified Protestants and Catholics. The leaders of the Catholic restoration, he said, were not prepared 'to go half-way to meet Protestantism in any of its objections, but rather to glory in those very doctrines that the Protestants had more forcibly, and sometimes, it must be admitted, most logically, repudiated'.[1] Clark also spoke of the vehemence of the Protestant rejection of Catholic imagery so that 'a new civilisation was created – but it was a civilisation not of the image, but of the word'.[2]

What occurred to me is that Anglicans and Catholics are more than two Communions or expressions of the Christian faith – they are two cultures. So the story I am to tell is not just about scripture and tradition, creeds and sacraments, liturgies and dialogues. It is a story about two peoples who have inherited a self-perception, and a view of the other, perhaps even a caricature. It seems to me that this duality was especially and quite forcefully evident in England; and was dispersed around the world wherever Catholics and Anglicans lived side by side. The 1960s mark the beginnings of the two communities addressing this precise issue of being two communions and two cultures.

When Bishop Mark Santer, on behalf of the Anglican

---

1 Kenneth Clark, *Civilisation*, London: BBC, 1969: 177.
2 Ibid: 159.

Communion, spoke at the Special Assembly for Europe of the Synod of Bishops in 1991, he said: 'Once separated, ecclesial communities develop different cultures which are extraordinarily difficult to reconcile – in, for instance, spirituality, in the way authority is exercised, and in the way the Christian community relates to the secular world.'[3] The precise problem, he says, rests not so much at the level of doctrine, but in the matter of the reconciliation of the people who hold the doctrines. The solution he proposes, and he speaks of it as being absolutely indispensable, is in the restoration of personal trust and friendship. 'When we speak of the Church as a communion of faith what we really mean is a communion of believing people.'[4]

This book begins at the point of two communions, two cultures. It portrays the mindset of each community, not in any deep scientific way, but simply and personally through the attitudes and words of Anglican and Catholic people. It watches them learning to be comfortable together, building friendships and searching out the ways and means of becoming one believing people.

In Chapter 1 a description of Anglicanism precedes a brief survey of earlier efforts at restoring unity. Friendship is identified as an important ingredient in the contemporary ecumenical scene, illustrated by the one that formed between Montini, later Paul VI, and a number of Anglicans. Chapter 2 reveals something of the depth of bad-feeling that prevailed in England for so long and the blockages that stood in the way of patient religious dialogue. A permanent Anglican representative, in the person of Bernard Pawley, was appointed to the Vatican and so Rome emerged as a place where friendships would build and dialogue could have a place.

The calling of the Vatican Council meant that a strong presence of observers would raise the consciousness among Catholics of the presence of other Christian communities in the world. Such is

---

3 'Address by Bishop Mark Santer, Delegate of the Anglican Communion, to the European Synod of Bishops'. *L'OR* 4 December 1991: 5.
4 Ibid: 5.

the subject of Chapter 3 where John Moorman, the leader of the Anglican delegation, is identified as one who had an especially influential role in building friendships among the observers and with Catholic bishops. Paul VI spoke his words of farewell to the observers quite sincerely: 'your departure will leave a loneliness around us'. Chapters 4 and 5 trace the history of the Anglican Centre from its founding in 1966 and the appointment of its first director, John Findlow, through to the present day. The final chapter offers a chronological overview of the work of the Anglican–Roman Catholic International Commission (ARCIC) and of the more recent body, the International Anglican Roman Catholic Commission for Unity and Mission (IARCCUM).

Acknowledgements

I wish to express my gratitude to those who made themselves available for interview. In particular I want to thank Mrs Margaret Pawley and Miss Virginia Johnstone who not only spent time with me, but rummaged in archives to find helpful documents. I am grateful, too, to Bishops Richard Garrard, Stephen Platten, John Satterthwaite, John Baycroft and John Flack for meeting with me. Mrs Kathryn Colvin, British Ambassador to the Holy See, Principe Jonathan Doria Pamphilj, Peter Rockwell, and Mrs Geraldine Tomlin and Marcella Menna of the Anglican Centre, and the staff of Lambeth Palace Library were very generous with their time. Finally, I wish to express thanks to a number of the clergy for their helpfulness, including: Revs Jonathan Boardman, Don Bolen, Stuart Burgess, Ronald Coppin, Merv Duffy, Barry Nichols, Bruce Ruddock, Tom Stransky and Michael Vono.

Frederick M. Bliss SM

Abbreviations

ACR	Anglican Centre in Rome (newsletter)
IARCCUM	The International Anglican Roman Catholic Commission for Unity and Mission
ARCIC	Anglican–Roman Catholic International Commission
CDF	Congregation for the Doctrine of the Faith
PCPCU	Pontifical Council for Promoting Christian Unity
PECUSA	The Protestant Episcopal Church in the United States of America
ECUSA	The Episcopal Church in the United States of America
SPCU	Secretariat for Promoting Christian Unity
WCC	World Council of Churches

I

Anglican Identity

Prior to the Second Vatican Council very few people in Rome apart from Giovanni Battista Montini, pro-secretary of state in the Vatican, knew much about the Anglican Communion. It was often the case that Anglicans were sweepingly categorized as among 'non-Catholics' and 'Protestants'. As time passed it was recognized that not only are Catholics baptized Christians, so too are Anglicans and most Protestant people, with all that baptism implies. Thus a new term was created – 'the separated brethren' – which allowed for distinctions to be made, but lent itself sometimes to an emphasis on the word 'separated', at other times on the word 'brethren', depending on who was speaking.

Surprising as it may seem, Vatican II occasioned a journey of discovery into Anglican identity, more or less paralleling the rediscovery among Catholics of their truer identity. What could be useful at this early juncture, therefore, is briefly to review the beginnings of the Church of England and the Anglican Communion, and the subsequent forces shaping them. The outcome will be a more informed appreciation of the Roman Catholic and Anglican traditions at work, as we shall observe them on the journey to the Vatican Council, and in its aftermath.

Though contacts between the Anglican Communion and the Catholic Church were taken up in earnest in the twentieth century, there were earlier attempts to retain and maintain contact between England and the Vatican, sometimes on a religious plane, at other times in diplomatic ways. Each of these will be briefly reviewed. This will be followed by some words on the two Anglican churches that have found a place in the city of

Rome. As a bridge to the second chapter the first will conclude with an examination of early twentieth-century informal conversations and friendships between Catholics and Anglicans that laid important foundations for more structured relations in the second half of the twentieth century.

The Church of England and the Anglican Communion

The beginning of the Church of England

It is known that there were enough Christians in the land to justify England having three episcopal representatives at the 314 Council of Arles. However, the English Church traditionally traces its origins back to Pope Gregory the Great (590–604). In 596 this missionary pope sent Augustine (Archbishop 597–605), the prior of his Roman monastery on the Coelian hill, along with forty monks, to re-evangelize England. Thus was founded the See of Canterbury in south-east England, of which Archbishop Rowan Williams is the 104th in succession to Augustine. Canterbury continues as the focal point of the Communion over the centuries.

The Church in England remained in communion with Rome until the sixteenth century, though at times amidst some tensions. On the eve of the English Reformation, for instance, one-third to one-fifth of the land was in the control of the church, disadvantaging both people and king. There was anger, too, at the outflow of taxes to the pope and disenchantment with the corrupt Cardinal Wolsey, chancellor of the realm. The situation worsened when he failed to secure Pope Clement VII's permission for King Henry VIII to divorce Catherine of Aragon.

Parliament and certain strategic appointments enabled the King to achieve his objectives. Beginning with the Acts in Restraint of Annates in 1532 and 1534, and a series of other acts climaxing in the Act of Supremacy 1534, the flow of taxes to Rome was discontinued. Papal authority was rejected and King Henry became 'the only supreme head on earth of the Church of England'. He married Anne Boleyn in 1533. His successors, young Edward VI and Mary Tudor, exposed England to the possibilities of a Protestant England or to the resumption of a Roman Catholic England. The end-product, if one can express it in such terms, was not a choice of one or the other, but a chasm between the Church of England and the Catholic Church, lasting into the twentieth century, felt even in the surrounds of the Second Vatican Council of 1962–5.[5]

The identity of the Anglican Communion

A variety of forces contributed to the evolution of the ecclesial identity of the Church of England, and later of the Anglican Communion.[6] An early hope was that *The Book of Common Prayer* and the Thirty-Nine Articles would underpin the Church of England as a 'bridge' between the Catholic and Protestant traditions.[7] But Thomas Cranmer (Archbishop 1533–53), viewed as the principal architect of the English reformation, demonstrated a marked sympathy for Zwinglian thinking, thus sending the church in a more reformed direction.[8] Later, and in a similar vein, the eighteenth-century evangelical movement, which also inclined to the continental preferences, favoured the doctrine of justification by faith, and an emphasis on scripture and preaching, conversion and holiness, with a corresponding de-emphasis on the sacrificing priesthood and the Eucharist.

By the end of the eighteenth century, evangelical urgency gave

---

5 Owen Chadwick, *The Reformation*, Harmondsworth: Penguin, 1964: 97–9.
6 Paul Avis, 'Keeping Faith with Anglicanism' in *The Future of Anglicanism*, Robert Hannaford, ed., Leominster: Gracewing, 1996: 8–10. Here Avis offers a brief survey of Anglican confessional identity based on the 1930 Lambeth Conference definition of the Communion.
7 Philip Turner, 'The "Communion" of Anglicans after Lambeth '98: A Comment on the Nature of Communion and the State of the Church' in *ATR*: 81, 1999: 281.
8 The 1552 Prayer Book and the Forty-two Articles of 1553 show the Reformed influences. See also Diarmaid MacCulloch's 'The Church of England 1533–1603' in *Anglicanism and the Western Christian Tradition*, Stephen Platten, ed., Norwich: Canterbury Press, 2003.

rise to the missionary movement, and that is when the 'Communion' came to exist.[9] Provinces were established around the world, and the need to maintain contact among them emerged. Hence, the first Lambeth Conference of 76 bishops of the Communion was held in 1867, a practice which continues every 10 years. The aim is to preserve and promote the unity of the Communion, which today comprises 38 provinces with a total membership of 78 million. At the third of these conferences, in 1888, the Chicago–Lambeth Quadrilateral was created as an expression of the unifying features of Anglicanism: the Holy Scriptures, the Apostles' Creed and the Nicene Creed, the two sacraments of Baptism and the Eucharist, and the historic episcopate.[10]

Shaping the Church of England and the Anglican Communion

Three men were the principal agents in the shaping of the Anglican Church. Matthew Parker, the Archbishop of Canterbury (1559–75), a true devotee of the *via media* and a contributor in the construction of the Thirty-Nine Articles, was important in designing the Church's identity. But it is the theologian Richard Hooker (1554–1600) who is widely regarded as the father of the Church of England. He resisted the efforts of some who set out to install only Calvinist thinking in the Church, and

---

9 See William Jacob's 'The Development of the Anglican Communion' in *Anglicanism and the Western Christian Tradition*, Stephen Platten, ed., Norwich: Canterbury Press, 2003. He explains that the development of the Communion cannot be viewed simply in terms of British colonial expansion. See also Colin Podmore's 'The Anglican Communion: Idea, name and identity' in *Aspects of Anglican Identity*, London: Church House Publishing, 2005: Chapter 3 where he details the relative recency of the term 'Communion' and offers reasons why the term 'Anglican' and 'Anglican Communion' are not used in formal expressions of Church of England identity.

10 Stephen Platten, *Augustine's Legacy: Authority and Leadership in the Anglican Communion*, London: Darton, Longman and Todd, 1997: 32–3.

prepared the classic Anglican theology, *The Laws of Ecclesiastical Polity*. In writing this book, Hooker was much influenced by his teacher, John Jewel (1522–71), Bishop of Salisbury, who had written *An Apology of the Church of England*.

In summary it could be said that Jewel related the Church more to its Catholic roots, and Hooker related it to the Puritan influences of the times.

Thus emerged the Church of England's hallmark: the *via media*. The Church is 'catholic', retaining the essentials of the early Church; the Church is 'reformed', without the excesses of medieval times; and the Church is '*troika*', acknowledging the necessity of scripture, tradition and reason, in contrast to the Protestant reliance on scripture alone. A critical edition of Hooker's works appeared in 1836, and it seems that it was then the term 'Anglicanism' was coined.

The preference, theoretically or theologically, was for a Church that was a 'bridge' or a 'via media'. The evangelical thrust proved to be a challenge to this middle way. Later, a nineteenth-century counter-challenge asserted itself, associated with the Oxford Movement, under the influence of John Henry Newman (1801–90). It sought a catholic revival, in opposition to the evangelical 'protestantizing' of the Church. The outcome was the rise of the Anglo-Catholics, one of whom – William Palmer – developed the 'branch theory', situating the Church of England in the company of the Catholic and Orthodox Churches, as three equal but distinct branches in the one, holy, catholic and apostolic Church.[11] Notably absent from the 'branches' were the Protestants, by then a sizeable number among the world's Christians.

---

11 Vincent Strudwick, 'Towards an Anglican Understanding of the Church' in *Is the Anglican Church Catholic?* London: Darton, Longman and Todd, 1994: 7.

The Role of 'Communion' Today

In Anglicanism today, the prevailing self-understanding among provinces, dioceses, parishes and individuals is that they all belong to the one, holy, catholic and apostolic Church. At the same time there is a variety of expressions of Anglicanism in the lives of people and communities, more or less following the patterns that emerged in the overview just completed.

The present age introduces a number of pressures that challenge the traditional expressions of unity. These are found, for instance, in movements sympathetic to increased decentralization, in worship conducted according to locally adapted prayer books, in the women's movement – particularly the ordination of women, and the admission to the priesthood and the episcopate of actively gay people. In the face of such stresses the Anglican Church is relying even more emphatically on the notion of 'communion', though undefined, in order to maintain the essentials of Christian unity. These expressions of diversity by the self-governing churches test the traditional Anglican instruments of unity, viz. the Archbishop of Canterbury and the Lambeth Conference, and more recently the Anglican Consultative Council since 1968 and the Primates' meeting since 1978.

None of these instruments carry 'legislative' power with respect to the member churches. Nevertheless, each has a level of 'moral' authority that the worldwide community of Anglicans – being a Communion – acknowledges. For example, the Archbishop of Canterbury, though *primus inter pares*, is a significant moral force within the Communion. He occupies the most ancient metropolitan See, he calls the Lambeth Conference, chairs the meetings of the Primates and is President of the Anglican Consultative Council. In fact, being in communion with the Archbishop is a sign of membership of the Anglican Communion. The resolutions of the 10-yearly Lambeth Conferences of the bishops of the Anglican world, though not binding, not infrequently result in member Churches modifying their own canons in line with the Conference recommendations. The Anglican Consultative Council, comprising laity, bishops, priests and deacons, meets approximately every eighteen months to two years. The Primates' Meeting, which occurs between Lambeth Conferences, is a consultation on theological, social and international matters. Each of these instruments, in its own way, alerts provinces to contemporary world problems and to matters relevant to the unity of the Communion, and as such they are sources of considerable influence.

We shall see, as our story unfolds, how the actions and discussions of the Anglican Communion as a whole, and the individual provinces which comprise it, have an impact on Anglican–Roman Catholic relations worldwide. So, for example, the acceptance by the Anglican Consultative Council in 1990 that it could no longer afford to underwrite the costs of running the Anglican Centre in Rome, required a redoubling of efforts to ensure that the Centre continued its work as almost a 'sacramental sign' of Anglicans' commitment towards relations with the Roman Catholic Church worldwide. The Centre has been and continues to be a key diplomatic instrument in conveying the implications of internal actions and decisions to the Holy Father and to the Roman Curia.

This became clear in the reverse direction as later on in this account we follow the work of the Anglican observers at the Second Vatican Council. Increasingly it became crucial in the 1990s following the 1991 publication of the Vatican response to *ARCIC I: The Final Report* and the Church of England's decision, through its General Synod in 1992, to proceed with removing the bars to women being ordained to the priesthood. The ability of the Anglican Communion to respond in this way has become more sophisticated in recent years. Not only did the Lambeth Conference respond positively to ARCIC I in 1988, but individual Anglican provinces did so too, as indeed did Roman Catholic Episcopal Conferences from around the world.

As ecclesiology and ecumenical theology have developed, so has the sensitivity of both communions to consulting each other on further developments. So, for example, when the Church of England commissioned the Bishop of Rochester to chair a group looking at the issues raised by ordaining women to the episcopate, so the Roman Catholic Church and other non-Anglican churches were asked to respond to the findings of the report. The English and Welsh Bishops' Conference has sent a comprehensive and considered response to the Church of England. Similarly, in 2003, when issues of sexuality placed greater strains on relationships within the Anglican Communion, the Archbishop of Canterbury and the President of the Pontifical Council for Promoting Christian Unity set up a joint commission to reflect on these and other developments within the Anglican Communion. Already the Anglican Communion had discussed the possibilities of a *covenant* and *Council of Advice* for the Archbishop of Canterbury to help handle key issues within the Communion that will necessarily have an impact of open Anglican relationships with other world communions.

Monumental events of 2004

Two contemporary testing instances have created enormous problems for the Anglican Communion. The first is the authorization in May 2003 of a Public Rite of Blessing for same-sex unions by the Diocese of New Westminster in the Anglican Church of Canada. The second is the consecration on 2 November 2003 of Canon Gene Robinson as coadjutor bishop of New Hampshire in the Episcopal Church (USA). Robinson, a divorcee, lives in an actively gay relationship.

Reactions within Anglicanism to these two events elicited words such as 'impaired', 'broken', 'fractured' or 'restricted' communion from the primates of the populous global South, and from a number of other provinces and dioceses. The day after Robinson's consecration, Archbishop Rowan Williams spoke of the 'very serious consequences for the cohesion of the Anglican Communion', announcing that a Commission would examine 'these consequences in depth'.[12] The Lambeth

---

12   www.archbishopofcanterbury.org

Commission was required to report to the Archbishop of Canterbury by 30 September 2004, in time for the meeting of the Primates in Armagh, February 2005.

We will return to a consideration of the 'Windsor Report' of the Lambeth Commission, and the Communiqué of the Primates' meeting after a brief consideration of another initiative of Archbishop Williams.

IARCCUM sub-commission on ecclesiology

Archbishop Williams decided to engage with the Catholic Church over the crisis arising out of the events in North America. Given the existing level of *koinonia* between the two churches which, admittedly, yearns for greater visibility in these testing times, the Archbishop made an approach to Cardinal Kasper of PCPCU. Together they put in place an *ad hoc* sub-commission of IARCCUM that would reflect on the current situation in the Anglican Communion, specifically in the light of the 35 years of dialogue between the two communions. This move allowed the work of ARCIC to become part of the process of reflecting jointly upon the ecclesiological issues raised by the developments in North America.[13]

The *ad hoc* sub-commission presented its report to Archbishop Williams and Cardinal Kasper on 8 June 2004. The report first recalled the recognition by the two communions of the agreed-upon language of ARCIC I, namely the terms 'substantial agreement' or 'significant convergence' with respect to so many components of the Christian faith. It also referred to the Mississauga acknowledgement of the impressive degree of agreement in faith that already exists between the two communions, including those expressed in the documents of ARCIC II.

The sub-commission returned often to the 1994 Agreed Statement, *Life in Christ: Morals, Communion and the Church*, because the issues under discussion are of a moral nature. This particular Agreed Statement speaks of Anglicans and Roman

---

13 ACNS 3700/ACO/2 December 2003.

Catholics sharing 'the same fundamental moral values'. But 'Recent developments', the document says in n. 3, 'call into question the extent to which we in fact share a moral vision.' It cites the case of the New Hampshire ordination, giving rise to two important questions. The first is about morality, and the second – by way of consequence – is about ecclesiology or the nature of the Church, asking whether or not the Anglican Communion is able to sustain a consistent moral teaching?

The representatives of PCPCU expressed themselves frankly at the sub-commission meetings and their views were taken seriously. The first point they made was that in the past, even in times of difficulty, the Catholic Church never downgraded relations with the Anglican Communion and does not intend to do so in this present situation. But the Anglican Communion has now to make decisions of 'monumental ecclesiastical importance', including a determination of the meaning of the word 'Communion' and all that it should imply for the unity of the Provinces in the one Anglican body. The Pontifical Council members suggested a strengthening of the authority structures and of the instruments of unity within the Anglican Communion, and a search for the ways and means to handle 'the tendency towards divergence on matters of faith and doctrine'.

The Windsor Report

The Windsor Report of October 2004 is a lengthy document of four sections. In his Foreword to the Report, Archbishop Robin Eames, the chairman, acknowledged that dissent is not new to the Communion 'but it has never before been expressed with such force nor in ways which have been so accessible to international scrutiny'. The 'bonds of affection', regarded as an attribute of the Communion, and the instruments of communion and unity, are threatened both by the developments in North America *and* by the reactions to them. The Report unfolds as a realistic, honest and rigorous analysis of the situation the Communion is in.

The first two sections present a very useful description of a *koinonia* ecclesiology, very much in tune with the thinking of ARCIC. Thus, life in the Anglican Communion should be seen as a partnership in which 'no part of the church can ignore its life in communion with the rest' (23). Whereas the decisions about the ordination of women to the priesthood and the episcopate did involve all the instruments of unity in the process, the decisions in North America were made locally, without reference to the wider Communion. To make matters worse, these local decisions were reached despite what the Communion saw as 'the standard of Anglican teaching' on issues of human sexuality as expressed at successive Lambeth Conferences in 1978, 1988 and 1998 and as confirmed by the primates in 2003. Furthermore, there was disregard of the views of the dialogue partners of the Anglican Communion who see these 'developments as departures from genuine, apostolic Christian faith' (28). Quite noteworthy is the level of attention given by the Commission to the views of the Anglican Communion's dialogue partners. Section B considers the nature of shared Anglican life, noting that when a serious impediment intrudes the inevitable result is that the 'Communion is now less full than it was' (50).

Section C, 'Our Future Together', acknowledges both the virtue in dispersed authority and 'its inherent weakness' (97). Thus, much of the section is given over to an examination of the instruments of unity and of canon law. It concludes with the suggestion of an Anglican Covenant.

From early times in Anglican history it became apparent that mechanisms should be set in place by which 'the Churches could take common counsel' (98). These mechanisms are the four instruments of unity spoken of earlier. The recommendation of the Report is not in favour of any formal power being given over to the instruments of unity, but for a strengthening of their moral authority. For instance, the Archbishop of Canterbury in relation to the instruments of unity acts as an individual, not in a conciliar way. In order, therefore, to enhance his position a Council of Advice is suggested to assist him 'in discerning when and how it might be appropriate for him to exercise a ministry of unity on behalf of the whole Communion' (112).

Interestingly, the Commission uses uncharacteristically strong language when it suggests the adoption by all the Churches of an 'Anglican Covenant which would make explicit and force-ful the loyalty and bonds of affection which govern the rela-tionships between the churches of the Communion' (118). The Commission believes the case for adopting an Anglican Covenant is overwhelming.

Section D, 'The Maintenance of Communion', concludes the Report with a summary of the findings and a number of recom-mendations. Notable with respect to the consecration of Bishop Gene Robinson is a questioning of the interdependence of ECUSA as a member of the Anglican Communion (129). On 13 January 2005 the House of Bishops of ECUSA sent 'A Word to the Church' in which they expressed 'sincere regret for the pain, the hurt, and the damage caused to our Anglican bonds of affec-tion by certain actions of our church'. This was followed by a 'Statement of Acceptance of and Submission to the Windsor Report 2004' from a number of bishops.

Section D continues, saying that the approving of Rites of Blessings of same-sex unions is judged to be contrary to the clear and repeated statements of the instruments of unity and as such constitutes a denial of the bonds of communion (141).

Recommendations of the Primates' Meeting, February 2005

The primates, meeting at Newry in Northern Ireland 20–25 February 2005, noted the high measure of support for the recom-mendations of the Windsor Report in the 322 responses they had received from around the Anglican Communion. They also observed a serious undermining by the recent developments in North America of the standard of Christian teaching on human sexuality as expressed in the 1998 Lambeth Resolution 1.10. Some of their responses or resolutions, in relation to the Windsor Report, are as follows.

Sections A and B of the Report offer an authentic description of the Anglican Communion and of the principles by which it is governed and sustained. Anglican respect for the authority of scripture, and the exercise of 'autonomy-in-communion', are very significant factors in promoting a balance among the 38 provinces. The primates issued an invitation to all the provinces about their willingness to commit to an interdependent life as outlined in the report.

(1) While welcoming the proposal in Section C of an Anglican Covenant, the primates see it as very much a long-term process. They question the suggestions about the role of the Archbishop of Canterbury and of a Council of Advice, fearing the creation of an international jurisdiction which could override provincial autonomy. Surprisingly, they entrust the Archbishop of Canterbury with the task of exploring 'ways of consulting further on these matters'.

(2) The primates accept the principle in Section D concerning the universal nature of the ministry of a bishop, though they see it as practically impossible to arrive at a formal process of wide consultation in the election and confirmation of bishops. It is a matter that should remain at provincial level, they suggest.

(3) For an appropriate response to the recommendations of the Windsor Report, time needs to be given to ECUSA and the Anglican Church of Canada. Both were requested to voluntarily withdraw their representatives from the Anglican Consultative Council up to the next Lambeth Conference. For the June 2005 meeting of the Consultative Council in Nottingham, England, representatives from the USA and Canada were invited for the specific purpose of explaining the thinking behind the recent acts in their provinces. The decision of both the Americans and the Canadians was neither to fully participate in nor to withdraw from the Council, but to send delegates to be in attendance.

In reflecting on the Windsor Report and the primates' response, a question does occur. Given that provincial autonomy is such a highly regarded feature of the Anglican Communion, has it proved to be an important strength? The primates see it as non-negotiable whereas no. 42 of the Report admits that Anglicanism has not always fully articulated how authority ought to work, and that 'we have reached the point where urgent fresh thought and action have become necessary'. The Report is open to a restricting of the independence of the provinces for the sake of the Communion, but the primates are 'cautious of any development which would seem to imply the creation of an international jurisdiction which could override our proper provincial autonomy' (9). In fact, the primates are not encouraging of any structural changes.

What should be important to Anglicanism at this juncture is ensuring that in the future the Communion is seen to be just that – a Communion. Relying on the scriptures as the supreme authority is a strength, but not simply in terms of their reception since the Reformation within the Protestant and Anglican domains. Very interestingly, the latest ARCIC Agreed Statement, *Mary: Grace and Hope in Christ*, makes the point that the authors 'have drawn on the Scriptures and the common tradition which predates the Reformation and the Counter-Reformation' (Preface). If we are to speak of Archbishop Williams as the 104th successor of Augustine, then the governance of the Church now ought to reflect a respect for, and a reception of, scripture *and* the whole of tradition.

Anglican tradition witnesses to the exercise of 'power' by the Archbishop of Canterbury beyond the See of Canterbury, even beyond the British Isles. Beginning in the late eighteenth century, many overseas bishops were required to take an oath promising 'all due obedience' to the Archbishop of Canterbury and his successors. With the passage of time, however, a new language of primacy emerged, that of a primacy of honour but not of jurisdiction, which: 'as the twentieth century progressed, was increasingly to be applied to the See of Canterbury in respect of the whole Anglican Communion'.[14] One should reasonably expect, therefore, an openness among the primates to an examination of the pros and cons of restoring to Canterbury an international jurisdictional role for the sake of the Communion.

---

14 Colin Podmore, 'Primacy in the Anglican Tradition' in *Aspects of Anglican Identity*, London: Church House Publishing, 2005: 67.

Early Hopes of Reunion with Rome

T. M. Parker is of the opinion that had events unfolded differently, Henry VIII might have died in communion with the Pope. It was only during the reigns of his two children that the immediate prospects of reunion diminished. With James I on the throne (1603–25), a new Oath of Allegiance was put in place which did not deny the Pope's spiritual authority, though it denied him the rights of deposing or excommunicating the king. This action created a new milieu for dialogue, which happened in fact to be a controversial one between James himself, later aided by Bishop Lancelot Andrewes (1555–1625), and with Robert Bellarmine (1542–1621) on the other side. Continuing to talk, as we have come to learn, keeps channels open, even if the subject-matter becomes a matter of controversy. The words of Father James Brodrick, as quoted in Parker's article, make the point:

> What a strange, contradictory world it is that set these two men, Andrewes and Bellarmine, so much alike in the very texture of their minds and hearts, at loggerheads. Bellarmine found the controversy with King James totally against the grain, and Andrewes against his will and inclination found himself the chief controversialist of the English Church.[15]

The seventeenth century lent itself to dialogue, though the intervention of Puritanism opposed any contacts with the papacy and was deeply suspicious of any 'Catholicizing currents in the English church'. The outcome was a severe dampening of the efforts of any Anglicans who believed reunion of Christians was still a possibility. Nevertheless, during the time of Charles I (1625–49) and his zealous Catholic wife Henrietta Maria, exchanges did occur. In 1633 Sir Robert Douglas, as the

---

15 See Father James Brodrick quotation and footnote 27 in T. M. Parker, 'The Church of England and the Church of Rome from the sixteenth to the eighteenth century' in *Anglican Initiatives in Christian Unity. Lectures Delivered in Lambeth Palace Library 1966*, E. G. W. Bill, ed., London: SPCK, 1966: 62–3.

Queen's representative and with the approval of the King, went to reside in Rome, as did his two successors, in the hope that an understanding could be reached with the Pope.

Moving in the other direction, a number of papal representatives were given a variety of portfolios. All of them enjoyed very warm relations with the monarchy. An interesting character was the Benedictine Dom Leander Jones, who as a student at Oxford was a contemporary of William Laud, with whom he retained a friendship until his death. He made the point in 1634 that Rome was not well-informed on the nature of the Church of England, which was unlike the Protestant churches on the continent. He recommended 'an assembly of moderate men . . . out of a sincere desire for Christian union'. Disapproved of by Rome because of some of his recommendations, Leander was succeeded as representative in England by Gregorio Panzani, from late 1634 to 1637. Discovering that the king was sympathetic to Pope Urban VIII, Panzani recommended that the king should meet the Pope 'half way' over the oath, but this idea was rejected in Rome. There was in 1634 the publication of a work by Christopher Davenport, an English Franciscan, demonstrating the compatibility of the Thirty-Nine Articles and the decrees of Trent. As Parker points out, this work had a significant impact on the movement for reunion with Rome, inspiring also in the nineteenth century John Henry Newman's *Tract 90*.

Panzani's successor, Scotsman George Con, soon realized that neither Archbishop Laud nor the king could move closer to Rome in the face of an ever-increasing powerful Puritan presence in parliament. Thus the Oath of Allegiance would remain a stumbling block in Church of England–Catholic relations for a long time to come.

Finally, William Wake, who was Archbishop of Canterbury from 1716 to 1737, though critical of certain aspects of Catholic doctrine, spoke quite emphatically of the Anglican desire for reunion, identifying the beliefs held in common by Canterbury and Rome. He also became involved with the Sorbonne doctors L. Ellies Du Pin and Piers Girardin, who advocated reunion of the French Church with the Church of England. This plan, as T. M. Parker points out, was destined to fail because all it could possibly achieve was yet another schism in Christianity.[16]

Relations of a Diplomatic Kind

After these more deliberate efforts at rebuilding relations between Rome and England, only intermittent contacts occurred, except for the restoration of the Catholic hierarchy in England in 1850, Cardinal Wiseman being the first Archbishop of Westminster. Thereafter, occasional visits to Rome by members of the Royal Family or their representatives served to maintain some form of contact. In 1859 the Prince of Wales visited Pope Pius IX; in 1872 the Prince and Princess had a private audience with the same Pope and in 1887 the Duke of Norfolk, representing Queen Victoria, congratulated Pope Leo XIII on his golden episcopal jubilee. Since the 1920s, visits to Rome by members of the Royal Family have become regular events. Queen Elizabeth II, for instance, has met three Popes: Pius XII in 1951 when she was a Princess, John XXIII in 1961 and John Paul II on three occasions.

Interestingly, the first-ever resident diplomatic mission created by the British Crown to the Holy See was established by King Henry VII (1485–1509). Christopher Bainbridge was the first English ambassador, and Sir Edward Carne the last before the formal break in the reign of King Henry VIII. Carne returned to Rome in 1555 as Queen Mary's ambassador, after which he became Warden of the English Hospice (now the Venerable English College) rather than return to England when Queen Elizabeth was on the throne. He is buried in the Church of San Gregorio Magno.

Centuries later, in 1914, contact was re-established when Sir

---

16 Norman Sykes, *William Wake: Archbishop of Canterbury 1657–1737*, Vol. 1, London: Cambridge University Press, 1957. See Chapter IV for an account of the correspondence between Wake and the two Sorbonne doctors.

Henry Howard, a Catholic, led a mission to the Holy See to extend the congratulations of King George V to Pope Benedict XV on his election to the papacy. This mission remained in Rome for a double purpose – to explain Britain's reasons for entering World War I, and as a counter to Austro-Hungarian and German influences at the Holy See. His successor in 1916 was Count de Salis, also a Catholic, both of them enjoying the title Envoy Extraordinary and Minister Plenipotentiary. This mission was renewed annually until 1926 when it became a permanent Foreign Office post. Thereafter, the appointees were not Catholics but invariably Anglicans, the second in command being a Catholic. Nowadays, neither religion nor gender is taken into account when such appointments are made. In fact, the present ambassador, who took up his post in late 2005, is 35-year-old Francis Campbell, a Northern Ireland Catholic.

During World War II when Britain and Italy were enemies, Sir d'Arcy Osborne, the envoy, was able to keep lines of communication open, to the advantage of the churches and the people. Three days after Italy entered the war Osborne moved from the Legation into Vatican City, where he lived from 1940 to 1944, the only Allied diplomat who remained throughout the war, managing to maintain contact with London by way of a diplomatic bag through neutral Portugal. A small annex attached to the Convent of Santa Marta became both his residence and his office. Finding himself in cramped conditions and without a bath, he would go to Montini's[17] flat to bath and also to store his valuables. Eventually Santa Marta was renovated, but even so, Osborne wondered about the value of his work in such an isolated location. The Foreign Office managed to get a message of assurance through to him, that it considered having a representative at the Vatican of utmost importance, 'if only to

---

17 Giovanni Battista Montini worked in the Secretariat of State during the pontificate of Pope Pius XII; in the war years he was responsible for the Holy See's extensive relief work. In 1954 he was appointed Archbishop of Milan and in 1963 was elected Pope, taking the name Paul VI.

support the Pope's authority'. He developed a great affection for Montini as is recorded in his diary of 8 July 1940. It reads: '(Montini at tea). I like him enormously and greatly admire his qualities and his character. Among other things he has vision, courage, and a very nice dry wit. How he can work as hard and unceasingly as he does I cannot conceive.'[18]

Sir Peter Scarlett, in charge just before and during the years of the Second Vatican Council, did an extraordinary job, facilitating small group meetings of bishops and observers from Commonwealth countries so that they could become acquainted outside of ecclesiastical confines. In 1982, after John Paul II's visit to the United Kingdom in May of that year, full diplomatic relations were established between the United Kingdom and the Holy See, the Legation in Rome being upgraded to an Embassy; in London, the pro-Nunciature was upgraded to an Apostolic Nunciature in 1994. Sir Mark Heath was the first Ambassador Extraordinary and Plenipotentiary to the Holy See.

Mark Pellew, ambassador in Rome 1998–2002, articulated some reasons why the United Kingdom places a level of importance on having relations with the Holy See. He said: 'Through its network of nuncios, missionaries and religious orders, the Roman Catholic Church is one of the best informed organisations in the world.'[19] Further, the Vatican's twentieth-century opposition to Fascism and Communism, for example, and the present strong papal leadership on moral issues, including human rights, poverty and debt relief, are also matters of political importance to Britain. Kathryn Colvin, ambassador 2002–05, pointed to the valued support of the Holy See for the British Government's International Finance Facility whose aim is to enable countries of the world to reach millennium development goals by reducing poverty and improving education. Francis Campbell, when he presented his credentials to Benedict XVI on

---

18 Owen Chadwick, *Britain and the Vatican during the Second World War*, Cambridge: Cambridge University Press, 1986: 128.
19 Speech by the British Ambassador to the Holy See, Mark Pellew, at the *Centro pro Unione*, 26 February 2002.

23 December 2005, explained that the United Kingdom's commitment to fighting world poverty is solidly based on principles of social justice which 'takes much inspiration from Catholic social teaching'. He added that his government 'was heartened by the support of the Holy See for its final report on the Commission for Africa'.[20] He also named three themes at the heart of the relationship between the United Kingdom and the Holy See which, he said, are also central points of his ambassadorship: interreligious dialogue, Europe and international development.

The embassy does not have an ecclesiastical role; the Anglican Centre instead handles matters between the Anglican Communion and the Catholic Church. Nevertheless, the Ambassador, often by way of providing a forum or offering hospitality, facilitates the coming together of Catholics and Anglicans as well as representatives from other Churches and faith communities.

Anglican Churches in Rome

There was no such thing as a 'Declaration on Religious Freedom' *(Dignitatis Humanae)* in nineteenth-century Rome. In fact, when the papacy exercised both spiritual and temporal authority, the only regular places where Anglicans or Protestants could worship were on diplomatic premises or outside the city walls. The first known Anglican service using the Book of Common Prayer occurred on 27 October 1816 in the Via dei Greci 43, near the Piazza di Spagna. Here, Anglican priest Corbet Hue, an Oxford don, and a congregation of four gathered for worship. As their numbers grew this English community established a chapel in what was known as the 'granary', outside the city walls near the Porta del Popolo. It remained their place of worship for the next 60 years.

Some years later, on 20 November 1859 in the Palazzo Bernini on the Corso, the first public liturgy of the Protestant Episcopal

---

20 Francis Campbell, 'Diplomatic accord', *The Tablet*, 7 January 2006: 15.

Church of America was celebrated. This American community assumed the name Grace Church, and in 1869 found a home for the next seven years, interestingly enough, in the old granary next door to the English Chapel, outside the Porta del Popolo.

In 1869–70 the first Vatican Council defined the doctrines of primacy and infallibility. This strengthening of papal spiritual power matched, as it were, a sudden death of papal temporal power. The new Italian state rose up, the troops breaching the wall near the Porta Pia on 20 September 1870. The constitution provided for the protection of religious freedom, which immediately prompted both the English and American Chapels in 1870 to look inside the city walls for new premises.

Unbeknown to one another, both communities approached the same architect to design their churches: All Saints' for the English community and St Paul's Within-the-Walls for the American community. The man engaged was George Edmund Street, one of England's foremost architects who, on his death, was buried in Westminster Abbey.

St Paul's Within-the-Walls[21]

The land in Via Nazionale, formerly the vineyard of the Barberine nuns, was purchased from an Italian deputy, Calvo, for $18,500. In six years the construction of the first non-Catholic Church built within the walls was completed, the consecration taking place in 1876. Robert Jenkins Nevin, the first rector (1869–1906), changed the name from Grace Church to St Paul's Within-the-Walls. In 1872 the legislature of the State of New York created a church board, 'Trustees of St Paul's American Protestant Episcopal Church, Rome', which continues to hold the title to the property. The vestry in Rome oversees management, control and maintenance.

---

21 R. J. Nevin, *St Paul's Within the Walls: An Account of the American Chapel at Rome, Italy*, New York: Appleton, 1878. Also: Walter Lowrie, *Fifty Years of St Paul's American Church, Rome*, Rome: 1926. Also: Judith Rice Millon, *St. Paul's Within-the-Walls, Rome*, Roma: Edizioni Dell'Elefante, 2000.

It is a spacious church, adorned with mosaics by George William Breck and Sir Edward Burne-Jones, and 17 fine stained glass windows, made by the English firm of Clayton and Bell, telling the life story of St Paul.

An interesting aspect of this beautiful church's history is the long line of American artists and art collectors who aided its construction and who contributed to its adornment, some of them parishioners. Robert Jenkins Nevin was himself a discerning art collector who attracted talented artists and rich benefactors to the church. Generous givers at the time of building included New York merchant John David Wolfe (died 1872) and his daughter, Catherine Lorillard Wolfe (died 1882), who would leave her sizeable art collection to the Metropolitan Museum of Art. William Waldorf Astor, American ambassador in Rome (1882–5) developed a lifelong interest in ancient sculpture and art, even to building up a large collection. He and his wife, Mary Dahlgren, were generous givers to St Paul's, to include support of the construction of the rectory.

Very significant in one span of the life of the church was the Morgan family. Junius Spencer Morgan (died 1890), a Massachusetts-born banker, paid for the apse mosaic, the parish minutes saying he was given the right to select the artist, the British pre-Raphaelite artist Edward Burne-Jones. Morgan was a non-residential honorary vestry member of St Paul's. His son, John Pierpont Morgan (died 1913), with William H. Herriman, after the death of Junius, assumed the financial obligation for the west wall mosaics, the idea of the second rector, Walter Lowrie, and the work of George W. Breck, which were unveiled on Christmas day 1913. The Morgan grandson – also John Pierpont (died 1943) – continued the family support of St Paul's. William Herriman and his wife were especially active in the life of the parish, and besides jointly gifting the mosaics with the Morgans, they were responsible for the garden wall, the wrought iron fence and the gate, the ironwork having been designed by St Paul's architect, George Edmund Street.

Two artists intimately associated with St Paul's were George William Breck (died 1920), already mentioned, and Elihu

Vedder (died 1923). Breck, a mural painter by training, was a director of the American Academy in Rome, a vestryman of St Paul's and a close friend of the first two rectors, R. J. Nevin and Walter Lowrie (1907-30). In 1907 Breck designed a commemorative plaque in honour of Nevin, which continues to mount the sacristy door. It was a gift of Herriman. Vedder settled in Rome and became a vestryman of the Church. Though not a religious artist, he did prepare a scheme for a mosaic on the west wall, for which he was paid, but the commission was given instead to Englishman Edward Burne-Jones. Nineteen paintings and sculptures by Vedder and a number of American artists, including George Inness and John O'Brien Inman, were prepared for auction in the United States. The intention was to raise funds for St Paul's but the great Chicago fire of October 1871 intervened, and the charitable money was redirected to Chicago. Vedder made a name for himself, some of his allegorical creations being featured in the hallway of the Reading Room of the Library of Congress, Washington D.C.

Other major donors to St Paul's include Mrs Henrietta Tower Wurts and Mrs Hickson Field. It was Mrs Field, for example, who came to the rescue in the 1890s when funds for the Burne-Jones mosaics were drying up. Recently widowed, she paid for the *Annunciation* in memory of her husband, and an anonymous gift made the *Tree of Life* possible, in memory of Mary Eleanor Field. Elizabeth Field married Prince Brancaccio whose palace today houses the museum of Oriental Arts.

The First World War meant a significant decline in the number of American residents in Rome; the Second World War saw the closure of the church on 26 May 1940, the Swiss Legation acting as protector until the arrival of the 7th Army in mid-1943. St Paul's reopened later that year, and for the duration of the war it became a chaplaincy for the United States Army.

It was in an apartment at St Paul's that the first representative of the Archbishops of Canterbury and York to the Holy See, Canon Bernard and Margaret Pawley, resided with their two children from April 1961. Bernard would also become an observer at the Second Vatican Council. As Bernard's secretary, Virginia Johnstone recalls that the Pawley apartment was a focal point for the Anglican observers and others as well. Each week they gave a dinner party and the guests included bishops, diplomats and other observers and journalists. The food was cooked by Margaret Pawley in a tiny kitchen and transported upstairs. Cardinal Montini, a great friend of the Pawleys, was one of their guests. The Findlows lived here also, from 1965 until April 1966 when they moved to the newly established Anglican Centre in the Doria Pamphilj palace.

Peter Rockwell, a parishioner since 1962 and a sculptor and art historian with a particular interest in stone carving, has contributed to the artistry of the Church. All the garden sculptures are his work, including *Charity* (1981) which commemorates the ministry of Robert Pegram, a former assistant in the parish, and the crucifix (1982) which is dedicated to Wilbur Woodhams, a rector of St Paul's (1961–81).

In 2005, St Paul's is a busy parish of about 320, mainly international parishioners, and it is home to a very active Joel Nafuma Refugee Center.

Rectors of St Paul's Within-the-Walls[22]

1869–1906:	Robert Jenkins Nevin
1907–1930:	Walter Lowrie
1930–1934:	Theodore Sedgwick
1934–1939:	Samuel Tyler
1939–1940:	Appleton Grannis
1940:	Hiram Gruber Woolfe
1944–1945:	Joseph Lewis Brown, chaplain with US Army
1946–1954:	Hillis Lattimer Duggins
1954–1957:	Charles A. Shreve
1958–1960:	Gerardus Beckman
1961–1981:	Wilbur Charles Woodhams
1981–1984:	Douglas Ousley
1985–1991:	Edward Todd
1992– :	Michael L. Vono

---

22 As listed in Millon: 212–13.

All Saints'[23]

The English community opted for a site on a disused convent at the corner of Via Babuino and Via di Gesu e Maria. Demolition of the old convent revealed a very historic spot that required special checking before preparation of the site could continue. Eventually work was able to proceed, All Saints' being George Street's last commission, for he died shortly before the laying of the foundation stone. His son, Arthur Edmund, supervised the building through to its completion in 1887.

Funding was a problem, so much so that in 1883 London wanted to disband the project. But the chaplain, the Revd Canon Henry C. Wasse, would have none of that, and relying on his own resources gave low interest loans in order to ensure the completion of All Saints'. Even at his death in 1891 most of the loans were still outstanding. The church was opened Easter Sunday 1887, the spire being added in 1937. John XXIII told the chaplain that sometimes at night he would take up his binoculars and look at the Churches of Rome. 'When I do that, there is your little spire right in the middle of my window.'

At one point in the life of All Saints' a group of parishioners under Dr Gason decided to set up a rival congregation, engaging Antonio Cipolla to design their place of worship, Holy Trinity Church, located near Piazza San Silvestro. Forty years later it was demolished and the foundation stone for a new Holy Trinity was laid in 1913 near Porta Pia, in what is now called Via Romagna. As the number of worshippers reduced to around 20, Holy Trinity held its last service on 18 April 1937. Around 1948 the church was sold and demolished.

Returning to the story of All Saints' Church, we find that it was formally closed by the civil authorities on 3 June 1940, remaining so until 9 June 1944. A senior chaplain of the Forces, D. H. P. Priest, conducted services for 14 months in what was known as a Garrison Church. The *canonica* next door was partially repossessed to house the first post-war licensed

---

23 See website: www.Allsaintsroma.org

chaplain, Canon John Findlow, with his wife Irina and their family, from 1949 to 1956. Canon Findlow, as earlier indicated, would return to Rome in 1965 as the second representative to the Holy See of the Archbishop of Canterbury, and the first director of the Anglican Centre, when he took up residency in the apartment at St Paul's. All Saints' is home to a plaque in memory of him. It reads:

JOHN FINDLOW
CANON OF MALTA[24]
Chaplain of All Saints Church Rome 1949–1956
Representative of the Archbishop of Canterbury to the Holy
See and first director of the Anglican Centre, Rome,
1966–1970
Died in London May 14th 1970
We thank God upon Every Remembrance of Him as a True
Priest, A Humble Man of God and an Excellent Worker in the
cause of Christian unity. Michael Cantuar.

One of the major features of the Church's interior is the large number of memorial tablets that line the aisle walls. Amongst the notable parishioners and clergy so memorialized is Lady Sibyl Graham, the widow of a British Ambassador to fascist Italy, immortalized by Dame Maggie Smith in Zeffirelli's film *Tea with Mussolini*. An earlier tablet in bronze recalls Lt Col. J. W. Keen, an English soldier who fought with Garibaldi's 1000 in the campaign of 1860 to unify Italy, who was rewarded by the Savoy monarchy with a barony.

Among the most eccentric of the clergy with a memorial is Harry de Nancrede, an American honorary assistant priest who worked for All Saints' and, when awarded an honorarium by the parishioners, spent it on the Venetian bronze hanging lamps for the sanctuary. There was one worshipper, a Miss Hall, who is described as a perfect encyclopedia because of her detailed

---

24 It has been pointed out that the inscription on the plaque is mistaken and should read: CANON OF GIBRALTAR.

knowledge of the English nobility whom she spent hours watching in the Piazza di Spagna or the Villa Borghese. So excited was she on being spoken to by Prince Max of Baden that she decided to abandon watching the rich and famous, devoting all her spare time to royalty. On Sundays at All Saints' she would sit as near as she could to the Ambassador's pew, one eye on her prayer-book and the other on a Royal Highness, 'straining her old ear to catch the particular sound of the royal voice in the singing of the congregation, praying for the Royal Family in every land with the fervour of an early Christian'.[25]

Although less richly decorated than St Paul's, All Saints' houses a splendid set of stained glass windows executed by the well known British firm Clayton and Hall. Modern additions include a *Via Crucis* and a *triptych* of All Saints' for the Lady Chapel by the Russian-born artist Dolores Lubienska. The other outstanding feature at All Saints' is its historic organ. An extremely large instrument in Roman terms, it was built by the British firm Conacher in 1894, with a major overhaul by the Italian organ builder Mascioni in 1960.

In 2005 there are about 200 parishioners in this busy parish under the care of Father Jonathan Boardman who is also Senior Tutor at the Anglican Centre.

Chaplains of All Saints'

1828	Richard Burgess
1837	James Hutchinson
1850	Francis Blake Woodward
1866	John Hutton Crowder
1869	Arthur Thomas Whitmore Shadwell
1873	Joseph Brett Grant
1874	Thomas Childe Barker
1875	Henry Watson Wasse

---

25 Munthe, *The Story of San Michele*, London: John Murray, 1929/1938: 326–7.

1891	Frank Nutcombe Oxenham
1910	John Gardner-Brown
1916	Gilbert Holme Sissons
1920	Bernard Edgar Holmes
1924	Lonsdale Ragg
1930	William Thomas Farmiloe
1934	Joshua Goodland
1935	Hugh Aldersey Tudor
1936	Ariel Law Harkness
1947	Clifford Stickney Powers
1949	John Findlow
1956	Douglas James Noel Wanstall
1971	David Gordon Davies
1974	Edward David Murfet
1977	David Henry Palmer
1983	Bevan Wardrobe
1992	Peter Marchant
1994	Geoffrey Evans
1999	Jonathan Thomas Boardman

Early Twentieth-century Anglican–Catholic Contacts

Well into the twentieth century, official Catholic thinking about unity expressed little more than an invitation 'to return to Rome'. Examples include the invitations from Pius IX at the First Vatican Council and John XXIII at the Second Vatican Council. More productive, in hindsight, were the unofficial conversations, which achieved profitable exchanges of knowledge, and the building of cells of goodwill at the level of scholarship and at the grassroots.

It became very obvious in the early twentieth century that French Catholics were taking the Church of England seriously, more so than was ever the case in England. The English Catholic bishops attributed this to French naiveté and ignorance.

Gregory Dix, whose story we shall tell shortly, observed the increasing breadth of French religious thinking. Prophetic theologians in many parts of Europe, including men such as Yves Congar and Maurice Villain[26] in France, were listened to, so that new attitudes regarding the nature of the Church, and her relationship with other Christian communities, were developing. This was well before the Second Vatican Council. Catholic England was not blessed with theologians who thought along these lines, with the possible exception of Abbot, later Bishop, Butler.

Gregory Dix

Born in 1901, Gregory Dix joined the Anglican Benedictines of the Nashdom community in Berkshire. In September 1936 he was invited by some French Catholics to visit them, in particular Abbé Paul Couturier and the Trappists at Notre Dame des Dombes. He accepted, the memory of the visit remaining so vividly with him that a year later he wrote to Jesuit Maurice Bévenot (b. 1897), whom he had read but never met, inviting him to Nashdom Abbey. The purpose of the visit, Dix explained, was that together they could set up a series of meetings between Anglican and Catholic theologians.[27] Congar's book, *Chrétiens Désunis*, would set the agenda.

Bévenot responded in the affirmative, and remarked, 'if we start in the right spirit, whatever happens, we'll *all* be the better

---

26 In the summer of 1938, for example, Villain made a *voyage de reconnaissance* of the Anglican Church in England. He called on H. F. Fynes-Clinton, a friend of Lord Halifax of the Malines Conversations; he visited Nashdom monastery, forming a friendship with Dom Benedict Ley, the novice-master, with whom he visited two nearby women's monasteries where he found what he describes as 'that marvellous *Pietas Anglicana*'. He also met the Revd Spencer Jones, a pioneer in prayer for unity and a friend of Lord Halifax who, at the age of 80, was writing another book, never published in English but which Villain undertook to translate into French, appearing as *L'Eglise d'Angleterre et le Saint-Siege, propos sur la réunion.*
27 In an unpublished, undated script Peter Hebblethwaite devotes over 40 pages to the Dix–Bévenot exchanges.

for the meetings, and if God draws anything more concrete from them, it will be His doing'. Five Jesuits from Heythrop and five Anglicans met at Nashdom for two days in June 1938, the first Catholic–Anglican meeting since the famous Malines Conversations. It was a successful encounter, as the subsequent correspondence between the two reveals.

In a letter to Bévenot on 28 March 1941, Dix expressed his pleasure that Archbishop of Canterbury Cosmo Lang had accepted the Pope's five peace points. 'It has impressed our rank and file very much that the Pope is the leader and mouthpiece of *Christendom*, not just the Head of the Roman Catholics.' Yet, Dix was adamant, 'not Malines or Lyons', by which he meant that English Catholics should not be by-passed in ecumenical discussions. The Malines Conversations of 1921–5[28] had taken place 'over the heads' of the English and Welsh bishops. That, and the unrepresentative nature of the Anglicans, led to the post-war slogan of George Leonard Prestige, one of the first Anglicans to be semi-officially 'received' in Rome, 'No more Malines'.

Sword of the Spirit

Adrian Hastings[29] tells the story of the unexpected co-operative venture referred to by Dix. It arose out of a letter written on 21 December 1940 to *The Times*, carrying the signatures of Archbishops Lang and Temple, Cardinal Hinsley and the Moderator of the Free Church Federal Council, George Armstrong. The letter listed and supported the Pope's five peace points as the only sure foundation for European peace, adding a further five points taken from the 1937 Oxford Conference.

During 1940 a group of educated Catholic laypeople proposed to the Cardinal that action was required, given his radio address in which he said the only weapon capable of winning the bat-

---

28 Bernard Barlow OSM, *The Malines Conversations 1921–1925*, Norwich: Canterbury Press, 1996.
29 Adrian Hastings, *A History of English Christianity 1920–1985*, London: Collins, 1986: 392–400.

tle was the 'Sword of the Spirit'. The immediate follow-up was the launching at a meeting in Archbishop's House, Westminster on 1 August 1940 of the 'Sword of the Spirit'. Pamphlets were distributed, non-Catholics were encouraged to join, other churches and the government responding enthusiastically. Bishop Bell of Chichester, second chairman of the Council for Foreign Relations, was particularly enthusiastic. Hinsley was backed by his auxiliary, but by hardly any other bishops. In the north the Catholic hierarchy was especially suspicious of the movement – quite understandably, given the self-perception of the Archbishop of Liverpool, Richard Downey, who made it clear 'that I rule the north'. This indicated, of course, that neither he nor quite a number of the English Catholic hierarchy could cope with a movement which was lay, ecumenical, intellectually progressive, decidedly English and fairly upper class.

The Catholic lay-organized public meeting was held on the weekend of 10 and 11 May 1942. The blitz had occurred on the Saturday evening: London was badly bombed and the House of Commons destroyed. People struggled over heaps of rubble to attend the second day. The Cardinal gave the closing speech, Bell whispering to him 'Eminence, may we say the Lord's Prayer?' Hinsley stood and led the whole assembly: *Our Father* . . . This action earned the disapproval of his fellow bishops, for praying with heretics. No longer could non-Catholics belong to the Sword, an article appearing in the *Clergy Review* of April 1942 which argued that Catholics 'cannot work with our non-Catholic brethren on the ground that we are both Christians, or that we believe the same things. We have no common Christian ground.'[30] These words stirred Father Maurice Bévenot to reply that the presence of war had brought to the fore the fundamental question of co-operation. Baptism, he said, provides a common ground, and what is more, it leads to the life of supernatural grace, adding 'he would be rash indeed who denies it wholesale to our non-Catholic brethren'. He continued: 'in the ontological order as God sees it, there is after all

---

30 *Clergy Review* April 1942: 162.

a real common basis between us over and above our common humanity, and therefore a basis which may rightly be called "a common Christian ground" '.[31] Such thinking would take time to be received within the English Catholic world.

With the death of Hinsley in March 1943, the Sword lost its only protector. But his funeral, even then, was an ecumenical occasion. The Sword, the Cardinal, the laity and the funeral were all memorable. We should never underestimate the role of memory.

Building friendships

It is probably true to say that in the first half of the twentieth century, neither in the Church of England nor in the Catholic Church was there a widespread wish for improved relations between the two communities. It is equally true to say that a number of ecumenically minded people were emerging, particularly in the Church of England. But with whom could they engage?

They were forced to look beyond English shores, to Rome, where they met Giovanni Battista Montini. Two British Ministers to the Holy See, Sir Francis d'Arcy Osborne and his successor Sir Victor Perowne,[32] were numbered among his close friends. Montini had been in charge of internal church affairs since 1944 and pro-secretary of State from November 1952 to 1954.

Visitors from England included Herbert Waddams, George Leonard Prestige and John C. Dickinson. Waddams first wrote to Monsignor Charles Duchemin, Rector of the Beda College, advising of his wish to visit Rome in February 1948. He said: 'I want if possible to have some unofficial conversations with

---

31 Maurice Bévenot, 'No Common Christian Basis?' in *The Clergy Review* XXII, June 1942: 266–9. See also 'Christian Co-operation in England To-day' in *The Month* 178, 1942: 298–306.
32 Sir Victor Perowne died in Rome 8 January 1951 and is buried in Camp Cestio, the old cemetery for non-Catholic foreigners.

Churchmen there, and if you can put me in the way of anything of this kind I shall be extremely grateful.'[33] Duchemin in
reply spoke of a 'little society' at the Beda, called '*Sint Unum*',
whose object is to study and understand Anglicanism better, to
remove misunderstandings and to clear the path to further and
more positive relations. He added that it is entirely private and
unofficial – presumably in relation to the Catholic bishops of
England.[34]

As it turned out, Perowne was persuaded to arrange for
Waddams to meet with Montini, only to find that Montini had
the flu. Nevertheless, Montini got out of bed for the meeting,
later remarking how much he learned from the conversation
and expressing his pleasure that useful channels of communication had been opened up. 'Dialogue must rest upon the common
assumption that both parties are in some way bound to Christ,'
asserted Waddams, 'and that there is an area of agreement as
Christians on which both may stand.'[35] Beyond dialogue, he
called for common prayer and common activity. It was very
much his impression that he and Montini were 'in some way
bound to Christ', he had yet to experience that common stand
in England.

The second visitor, late in 1949, was George Leonard Prestige,
editor of the *Church Times* and Acting General-Secretary of the
Council for Foreign Relations. He was the first to test the waters
about possible conversations. Prestige came with a modified
blessing from Archbishop Geoffrey Fisher who, according to
Purdy, was keen to be informed but not to be involved.[36] He
was encouraged by Bishop David Mathew, former Auxiliary
of Westminster and then Apostolic Nuncio in Mombasa, one

---

33 Herbert M. Waddams. Letter of 6 January 1948, to Monsignor
Charles Duchemin. Lambeth Palace Library.
34 Charles Duchemin. Letter of 14 January 1948, to Herbert Waddams.
Lambeth Palace Library.
35 Ibid.
36 William Purdy, *The Search for Unity: Relations Between the
Anglican and Roman Catholic Churches From the 1950's to the 1970's*,
London: Geoffrey Chapman, 1996: 5.

considered unique among the English Catholic hierarchy of the time. Prestige visited Vatican offices and seminaries, and met Tisserant and Montini. It was the latter who 'impressed me most profoundly', remarked Prestige. Montini was anxious that Anglican–Catholic contacts continue, suggesting that, at this point, it might be better for the conversations to be outside England. Mathew wrote to Prestige: 'I am happy that everything went so well, and particularly that you liked Mgr Montini. He (and in a sense he alone) is the key to the situation. It is difficult to over-estimate his significance.'[37]

A third visitor was John C. Dickinson, a Fellow of Pembroke College, Cambridge. He wrote an undated report, but probably in late 1959 or early 1960, that he called 'The Italian Church'. It expresses his impressions of his visit to Rome following Bishop Bell's efforts at establishing unofficial contacts. He wrote: 'it is quite certain that there is present among instructed Italian churchmen a real and growing spirit of enquiry which manifests itself *inter alia* in real friendliness towards Anglicans they meet'.[38]

In 1950 a conversation began in Paris, comprising seven Anglicans and seven French Catholics, and there were two less enterprising efforts, one in Strasbourg later in 1950 and the other at Hampstead in January 1952. With Prestige's sudden death in 1955, new teams were arranged to continue the discussions. Meetings were held in Rome in 1957, Cambridge 1958 and Assisi in 1961. While the Catholic bishops in England continued to be suspicious of these various engagements, the religious orders were proving more and more helpful.

A friend of Montini in Rome was Father Charles Boyer SJ of the Gregorian University.[39] Present at the inauguration of the WCC in Amsterdam in 1948, it was very much Boyer's

---

37 George Prestige. Letter of 26 December 1949, received from the Most Revd David Mathew. Lambeth Palace Library.
38 John C. Dickinson in file 'Anglican Visitors to Rome 1959–1981'. Lambeth Palace Library.
39 Bernard and Margaret Pawley, *Rome and Canterbury Through Four Centuries*, London: Mowbrays, 1974: 321ff.

mind that the Catholic Church should not ignore the budding ecumenical movement. He was very happy to be a go-between for Anglicans wanting access to Montini. On the occasion of Archbishop Donald Coggan's visit to Pope Paul VI on 28 and 29 April 1977, the very ill pontiff was able to lead the Archbishop over to the seated octogenarian, Charles Boyer, and say: 'This is the man who made all this possible.' John Lawrence, in his 'Roman Diary', commented: 'I saw Père Charles Boyer, the head of the *Unitas* organisation. He is a little Frenchman with a clever, sensitive, spiritual face. He is very friendly, but he is the prisoner of a theology which is bursting at the seams.'[40] A model prisoner he remained, it would seem, never arriving at a perception of ecumenism beyond the 'return' model.

Anglican house guests in Milan

In November 1954 Montini was appointed Archbishop of Milan; the year following he was visited by George Bell of the Anglican Council for Foreign Relations. The Pawleys record that the two men took an instant liking to one another, Bell remarking: 'I was never more impressed, even by my friends among bishops in the north of Europe, than by that man's desire to learn.' Montini then took an initiative: he would welcome a group of Anglicans as his guests in 1956.[41]

Bell was a remarkable man.[42] In his younger days, two bishops influenced him profoundly, imparting a vision that stayed with Bell all his life. The first was Archbishop of Canterbury Randall Davidson (1903–28), for whom Bell worked a number of years, accompanying the Archbishop when he addressed the 1910 World Missionary Conference in Edinburgh, widely regarded as

---

40 John Lawrence, 'Roman Diary' February–March 1959. In file 'Anglican Visitors to Rome 1959–81'. Lambeth Palace Library.
41 Bernard and Margaret Pawley, *Rome and Canterbury Through Four Centuries*, London: Mowbrays, 1974: 327–8.
42 George Slack, *George Bell*, London: SCM Press, 1971. Also: Ronald C. D. Jasper, *George Bell: Bishop of Chichester*, London: OUP, 1967.

the beginning point of the modern ecumenical movement. The Nikæan Club was founded under Davidson's auspices in 1925, marking the 16th centenary of the First Ecumenical Council of Nicaea, 325. The club continues 'to further relations with non-Anglican Christian Churches, to assist students from such churches and to offer hospitality on behalf of the Archbishop of Canterbury to representatives of such churches'.[43] Currently there are 350 members, each of them having been elected, their ecumenical credentials important in the process.

The other man was the 1930 Nobel Peace prize-winner, Lutheran Archbishop Nathan Söderblom of Uppsala, sometimes spoken of as the father of the ecumenical movement. As Kenneth Slack remarks, just as World War I moved Söderblom to bring 'Life and Works' into being, becoming its leader, so World War II pushed Bell into continuing it, and becoming also a prime mover for the formation of the WCC, transcending all human divisions. While Life and Works remained an abiding interest for Bell, later he said, given the chance again he would have reversed the order in favour of 'Faith and Order,' a body whose aim is principally contributing to the 'shaping' of the Church.

Bell, though not responsible for organizing the visit to Milan, recommended acceptance of the invitation. In 1956, Archbishop Montini became host for ten days to four priests and one layman. They were J. C. Dickinson of Pembroke College, Cambridge, later lecturer at Birmingham; Prebendary C. L. Gage-Brown; Colin James, later bishop of Winchester; Colin Hickling, of Chichester, a layman; and Bernard Pawley, eventually the Archbishop of Canterbury's representative to the Holy See. John Moorman, who was originally selected to lead the group, was prevented from attending because of the sudden death of a relative, though he did become a lifelong friend of Montini. Two Catholics were present, Charles Boyer SJ and Sergio Pignedoli, who spoke English well and had a good sense

---

43 The Nikæan Club. Nomination Form for Membership. Lambeth Palace Library.

of humour, dining regularly with the visitors. Montini joined them for meals on three or four occasions.

Montini's interest in England and Scotland dates back to his visit there in the summer of 1934. Twenty years later he recalled vivid memories of Durham Cathedral, and indicated his continuing interest in Anglican Church music, collecting records and tapes of it. Now he was intent on extending his knowledge, by discovering who Anglicans are from what they say about themselves. As the Anglican observers of Vatican II testify, he never lost his interest in and affection for them.

On 12 December 1956, Archbishop Geoffrey Fisher wrote a letter of thanks to Montini. He said: 'I am sure that such personal contacts as were enjoyed during this visit are the best way of creating that spirit of love and understanding between members of different theological traditions which is a prerequisite for closer unity in the future.' Montini replied on 19 December: 'I express the wish that the spirit of charity and the love of truth may produce even better fruits in the future. To this wish – today, the feast of St Thomas of Canterbury – I add a special prayer.'

Pawley, Dickinson and Hickling all stayed in touch, before and after Montini became Pope in June 1963. Hickling regularly sent Christmas cards until Mgr Jean-Francois Arrighi of the Secretariat for Promoting Christian Unity[44] (SPCU) pointed out that the receiving of cards was not an Italian custom; a Christmas letter would be more appreciated. Thereafter, Hickling wrote newsy Christmas letters. Gage-Brown left a long report, entitled *Visit to Milan*, intended in the first place for the Archbishop of Canterbury. Montini, he wrote,

> was genuinely anxious to promote friendly contacts. When asked whether we could talk about our visit in England, he replied that we could say, what was indeed the truth, that it was simply a visit of friends. We said as tactfully as possible

---

44 The Secretariat for Promoting Christian Unity was established by John XXIII on 5 June 1960.

that relations with the English Roman Catholics were not particularly friendly, and I said this could be understood by our persecution of them in the past, to which he replied that such history should be forgotten.[45]

Within three years of the Anglican visit, John XXIII became Pope and summoned an ecumenical council. The Catholic bishops of the world were asked what should be on the agenda. Montini put ecumenism first, offering Milan as a place for conversations with Anglicans. In 1960, alluding to Dom Lambert Beauduin's Malines formula of 'united but not absorbed', Montini wrote: 'Other Christians separated from the unity of the Church must be given the hope of returning with dignity . . . one should show a special indulgence in matters of rites and discipline.'[46]

The Archbishop of Canterbury was kept informed, and this is perhaps a reason why, when the possibilities for direct official contacts opened up with John XXIII, the Anglican Communion was the first to respond.

45 William Purdy, *The Search for Unity: Relations Between the Anglican and Roman Catholic Churches From the 1950's to the 1970's*, London: Geoffrey Chapman, 1996: 19.
46 Reference as supplied in Hebblethwaite's unpublished manuscript is to *Discorsi e Scritti sul Concilio 1959–1963*, Brescia, 1983: 34.

2

Mid-twentieth Century England and Rome

It had been recognized for quite a while that England was not the place for Catholics and Anglicans to begin the process of healing memories. Rome, an interesting choice, turned out to be just right. If there were bad memories, the eternal city was able to provide an altogether different perspective on them, and facilitate healing. An important ingredient in all this was friendship, as this chapter will tell. John XXIII and Archbishop Fisher met and liked each other. Bernard Pawley enjoyed the Pope and formed firm bonds with Augustin Bea[47] and Jan Willebrands.[48] Giovanni Battista Montini cherished close friendships with any number of Anglicans.

In England tensions persisted, including serious stereotyping of one another. It was deeply felt to the point where many of the Catholic bishops of England were threatened by the presence of competent Anglican observers at the Council, partly because the bishops – in Eamon Duffy's estimation – 'were practical men for whom theology was a bore'.[49] It was inevitable that the English Catholic hierarchy would not make a good showing at Vatican II.

---

47 Bea was born in 1881 in Germany. He was made cardinal 14 December 1959 and bishop 19 April 1962.
48 Willebrands was born in 1909 in Holland. He was made bishop 4 June 1964 and cardinal 28 April 1969.
49 Eamon Duffy, 'Tradition and Reaction: Historical Resources for a Contemporary Renewal' in *Unfinished Journey. The Church 40 Years after Vatican II*, Austin Ivereigh, ed., London: Continuum, 2003: 53.

Bernard Pawley's Appointment to Rome

Early in 1961, the year Michael Ramsey became Archbishop of Canterbury, the *Church Times* jumped the gun on the Press Office at Lambeth Palace. The paper announced the appointment of Canon Bernard Pawley, Treasurer of Ely Cathedral and Proctor in the Convocation of Canterbury, as the permanent personal representative of the Archbishops of Canterbury and York to the Holy See.

Bernard and Margaret arrived in Rome on 13 April 1961. They relied on Bernard's Ely salary and a grant of £2,000 from a voluntary society, intended to last two years. Their arrival surprised both the SPCU and the British Legation to the Holy See, since neither was officially informed of their arrival. The Italian press was fascinated at this young cleric with wife in hand, who spoke Italian '*abbastanza bene!*' The Pawleys took up residence in a flat at St Paul's Within-the-Walls, the American Episcopal Church on Via Napoli, where a widely respected Wilbur Woodhams was the chaplain.

From the very beginning Bernard Pawley was intent on defining his task. He explained to a meeting of *Foyer Unitas*[50] that the eventual aim of the Archbishops of Canterbury and York was not duality or peaceful co-existence with Catholicism, but unity, understood as an absolute term.[51] Detecting a movement in Catholic thinking, Pawley studiously worked his way through two years of *La Civilta Cattolica* to get a feel for the growing sense of the spirit in Catholicism. He was impressed by Hans Küng, whom he met on a number of occasions, and by Küng's *The Council and Reunion* as representing the best

---

50 *Foyer Unitas* was an international body of clergy and laity founded in Rome in 1945, by Father Charles Boyer SJ in association with a group of professors, writers and clergy. Its purpose was the promotion of Christian unity, and a practical aspect of this work – in conjunction with the Ladies of Bethany – was welcoming to Rome Christians of other traditions, conducting tours for them and arranging audiences with the Pope.

51 Pawley report 11: 9 June 1961.

of forward-looking Catholic thought, particularly Küng's state-ment that 'Reunion will neither be a Protestant return nor a Catholic capitulation, but a brotherly approach on both sides.'[52] Margaret Pawley, who liked Küng, observed nevertheless that he was an angry young man. Yves Congar found Küng impa-tient and too radical in his demands.

Pawley came up with a plan. The first task was to put 'union' into practice at the level of charity. Doctrinal union, he com-mented, is more difficult and will require a special grace. His second task was to meet with theologians and observe their attempts to read the signs of the times against the background of long traditions. And his third task was to become acquainted with Vatican officials.[53]

Bernard was meticulous in his reporting to the Archbishop of Canterbury on his dealings with the SPCU and other Vatican offices, and on the debates at the council. He and Margaret cultivated an immense range of contacts and friends, and often enough they found mention in his more than 160 written reports to the Archbishop. This chapter, therefore, will turn often to these papers since they represent another view of the sixties in Rome and in relationships between the two communions.

The Roman Milieu

The years 1961–2 witness the beginnings of Anglicans and the Vatican becoming comfortable with one another. It was as if two hitherto 'unknowns' pondered how to relate, as this little story illustrates. A small Anglican delegation was leaving the Vatican through the *Sala Clementina,* following a meeting with John XXIII. They passed two cardinals and not less than twenty bishops and *monsignori* waiting for their audience, and Pawley noticed how these prelates tried, though not very successfully, to give an ecumenical smile.[54]

---

52 Pawley report 15: 25 September 1961.
53 Pawley report 7: 18 May 1961.
54 Pawley report 23: 21 November 1961.

In its effort at becoming comfortable with the presence of an official representative of the Archbishop of Canterbury on its doorstep, the Vatican's newly established SPCU sought to 'justify' Pawley's presence. Secretary Willebrands found a 'loophole' provided by the encyclical *Ad Petri Cathedram*[55] that those separated from the Holy See are offered a gentle invitation to seek and to follow that unity which Jesus Christ implored from his heavenly Father.[56] The general Catholic perception of 'unity' was defined by Pius XII in his two encyclicals *Mystici Corporis Christi* of 1943 and *Humani Generis* of 1950. These papal statements provided the substance of the document on the Church which was prepared for the forthcoming Vatican Council, stating that 'the Roman Catholic Church is the Mystical Body of Christ . . . and only the one that is Catholic has the right to be called Church'.[57]

One would expect a degree of wonderment on the part of Catholics at an official Anglican presence in Rome, and a level of resentment among Anglicans at the persistent and exclusive ecclesial self-perception of Catholics. Beyond wonderment and resentment there was a serious and growing questioning of this Catholic exclusivity. Such questioning turned into a movement. The impact of this movement was first felt outside official Catholic circles, but it soon became the prompt that gave rise to the Second Vatican Council. Ecclesiastical leaders, including Pius XII and his successor, were almost certainly aware of it, though they did not know how to define or handle it. Pius XII wrote his encyclical *Humani Generis* in an attempt to respond to the times; John XXIII's choice was to call a council.

Despite the forthrightness of the ecclesial claim of Pius XII, the very title he gave to the June 1943 encyclical, *Mystici Corporis Christi*, laid the foundations for a rediscovery of the biblical and

---

55 Encyclical of 29 June 1959.
56 Pawley report 2: 19 April 1961.
57 See Gérard Philips, 'History of the Constitution' in *Commentary on the Documents of Vatican II*, Vol. I, London: Burns and Oates, 1967: 105–37.

patristic understandings of the Church. What is more, *Divino afflante Spiritu* of September 1943 allowed scholars to employ modern historical methods in their study of the scriptures, in effect to discover what the Church looked like in its beginnings. Maybe other Christians were better able to perceive what was actually happening than were Catholics, hence J. N. D. Kelly's assessment of Pope Pius XII that after his death in October 1958 'his moral authority probably stood higher in non-Roman than Roman circles'.[58] Herbert Waddams of the Council for Foreign Relations observed that:

> He never ceased to give attention to relations with other Christians. (Instance G. Bell's visit.) During the past fifteen years or more there had been distinct change for the better in relationships and much greater readiness on both sides for Christians to see each other. For this development, which must be a cause of thankfulness to all Christians, the late Pope was in considerable measure responsible.[59]

John XXIII, and Paul VI in the early years of his pontificate, were also the inheritors of a long tradition that espoused *Extra Ecclesiam nulla Salus,* which was understood to mean 'Outside the Roman Catholic Church there is no salvation.' Yet they were aware of the twentieth-century enquiries about 'salvation' and 'justification', about 'grace', 'church' and 'church membership', and so many other questions. They were aware of the work of competent scholars and sincere prophetic figures questioning and challenging the traditional explanations. It was a time when there were more questions than answers, leaving these Popes with little option but to follow the traditional lines. Nevertheless, they pondered all the while, searching for answers, as their biographies testify.

---

58 J. N. D. Kelly, *The Oxford Dictionary of Popes*, Oxford: Oxford University Press, 1986/1991: 320.
59 As quoted in William Purdy, *The Search for Unity: Relations Between the Anglican and Roman Catholic Churches from the 1950's to the 1970's*, London: Geoffrey Chapman, 1996: 23.

The Election of John XXIII

In October 1958 Angelo Giuseppe Roncalli, the Patriarch of Venice, was elected Pope. Given his age, John XXIII was considered both a stop-gap and a guarantor of the traditional line. He was a very traditional bishop, but he was also shrewd, sensing that the Church needed change. He did not understand what exactly it needed – simply that *aggiornamento* was required. Thus, 90 days into his pontificate, on 25 January 1959, John XXIII summoned a general council, which began on 11 October 1962 and which, in the Pope's estimation, would conclude before Christmas. In fact, it lasted four years.

John XXIII's approach was amazingly simple, as Bernard Pawley was to discover at his first audience in 1961. The Pope asked very human questions.

'Are you married?'

'Yes.'

'Well, that need not divide us, so was St Peter. Parents still alive?'

'Yes.'

'Are they very old?'

'No, only in their seventies.'

'Are you a theologian? . . . Nor am I. It is theologians who have got us into the mess, and we have to get ourselves out; it is practical men like you and me who will deliver us from it.'

Peter Hebblethwaite's assessment is that Angelo Roncalli's experience in Bulgaria, Turkey and France taught him that counter-reformation attitudes were outdated. His goodness and spiritual intuition transforming those hitherto regarded as 'heretics', 'schismatics' or at best 'dissidents' into 'separated brethren'. And he deplored the separation.[60] The night before the council, when he learned that the observers were to be seated distant from the altar, he insisted that they be moved in front of the boxes allotted to the diplomatic corps, where they could properly do what they were there for: observe.

---

60 Peter Hebblethwaite, *In the Vatican*, Bethesda: Adler and Adler, 1986: 147.

Spiritual renewal and pastoral updating were his immediate aims, with Christian re-union somewhat more remote. Once the Catholic Church had renewed herself, he explained to Pawley, the council would be able to say to other Christians: 'Here is your mother church, all resplendent and beautiful: now surely you will want to find your way back.' He never changed on this, though the words he used to speak of 'non-Catholic' Christians became more and more sensitive, in tune with what John Moorman recognized as John's 'charismatic personality'. It is very interesting, too, that Pawley observed from quite an early date, perhaps within a month of his 1961 arrival in Rome, that John XXIII was 'working uphill . . . trying to ward off possible criticisms . . . I wish I could report what was at the back of the Pope's mind.'[61] He had come across a man, anchored in tradition, though endowed with an extraordinary openness to an unknown future.

This openness was again surprisingly revealed on 30 May 1960, when John XXIII announced his intention of establishing a Secretariat for Promoting Christian Unity (SPCU).[62] Its immediate purpose was to provide information to non-Catholics, to receive and assess their wishes before transmitting them to the council and to aid them in their journey to unity.[63] The appointments to this body were inspired: Father Augustin Bea, the Jesuit rector of the Biblical Institute, as president, and Father Jan Willebrands as secretary. The office opened at Via dei Corridori on 24 October 1960, the first meeting of officers and consultants taking place three weeks later. In a matter of months it became almost certain that the Secretariat would become a permanent body, and so it did in 1966.

---

61 Pawley report 6: 7 May 1961.
62 In virtue of the Apostolic Constitution *Pastor Bonus* of 28 June 1988 the Secretariat was upgraded, as from 1 March 1989, to the status of a Council, being named the Pontifical Council for Promoting Christian Unity (PCPCU).
63 Pawley report 3: 22 April 1961.

Visit of Archbishop Fisher to Rome

Anglican Bishop Mervyn Stockwood of Southwark, at an audience with John XXIII, was taken aside, the Pope asking him to convey this message to Archbishop Fisher: 'Two souls can meet in prayer though distance divide.' Stockwood duly delivered it in April 1959, the Archbishop responding that a context for a visit to Rome did present itself, namely, the creation of the SPCU and the proposed Vatican Council. Fisher immediately planned his journey to include Istanbul, Geneva and Rome, covering all bases, as it were.

Being a 'low churchman',[64] Fisher (1945–61) was not well-disposed to Rome. 'I grew up with an inbred opposition to anything that came from Rome. I objected to their doctrine; I objected to their method of reasoning; I objected to their methods of operation in this country. So I grew up, and I saw no reason for differing from that opinion as the years went by.'[65] His preference, in terms of relationships, was to move closer to the Methodists at home, and with non-Roman churches abroad. He was not at all fussed about the sort of doctrinal agenda that might preoccupy Catholics. In Fisher's opinion problems among churches would blow away; it was a matter of getting along together.

The visit could have turned into a total disaster, had a dictatorial curia got its way. Even so, Cardinal Domenico Tardini laid down four conditions regarding the visit, which he sent to Sir Peter Scarlett, the British Minister to the Holy See. (1) No official photograph of Dr Fisher with the Pope. (2) No visit to Bea, the head of the SPCU. (3) No press release after meeting with the Pope, and (4) the Minister may not invite any Vatican official to his house in order to meet with Archbishop Fisher. Adding insult to injury, only a very brief notice appeared in *L'Osservatore Romano,* indicating that Dr Fisher (not 'Arch-

---

64 Owen Chadwick, *Michael Ramsey: A Life*, Oxford: Clarendon Press, 1990: 314.
65 Quoted in Adrian Hastings, *A History of English Christianity 1920–1985*, London: Collins, 1986: 522.

bishop') had had an audience with John XXIII. As the Rome correspondent of *The Times*, Peter Nichols observed, 'The visit was treated like a guilty secret.'

On that 2 December morning in 1960 Archbishop Fisher said: 'Your Holiness, we are making history.' The Archbishop later reflected: 'I did not have to create an atmosphere of friendship. I walked straight into it. We talked like two good Christian gentlemen about anything that came into our minds.' When the Pope mentioned the separated Eastern and Protestant Churches, the Archbishop explained that Anglicans fell into neither of these categories. When John XXIII spoke of the return of the separated brethren to the Mother Church, the Archbishop said: 'Your Holiness, not *return*! None of us can go backwards. We are now running on parallel courses; we are looking forward until in God's time, our two courses approximate and meet.' After a moment's pause the Pope said: 'You are right.' In the course of the conversation the Archbishop thanked John XXIII for establishing the Secretariat under Cardinal Bea. The Pope smiled and said, 'Yes, and this afternoon you shall see Cardinal Bea.' [66] Tardini had been overruled.

In the afternoon the Archbishop met Cardinal Bea at his residence, the Brazilian College. It was agreed there, in the words of Monsignor Willebrands, that the Archbishop's presence would be continued in Rome 'by sending a representative of the two Sees of Canterbury and York . . . to follow very closely the preparatory work of the Council.'[67]

Three Friends

Bernard Pawley not only admired Cardinal Bea and Monsignor Willebrands; they became his close friends.

At his first official meeting with Cardinal Bea on 1 May 1961

---

66 Quoted in William Purdy, *The Search for Unity*, London: Geoffrey Chapman, 1996: 30–1.
67 Speech by Mgr J. G. M. Willebrands at the Inaugural Meeting of the Anglican Centre in Rome on 5 October 1966.

Pawley was assured that the Pope was pleased with his assignment. There was no need to be furtive.[68] Pawley developed a great admiration for Bea, whose honesty he liked, an example of it being expressed in an interview the Cardinal gave to *France Catholique*:

> We Catholics owe a duty to Protestants . . . We failed them badly in the 19th century when they fell prey to many secularist ideas. Protestants, who are not alone responsible for splitting the Church, can also aspire to salvation on a level footing with Catholics. In a certain manner they are also united to the Church, and we Catholics should do all we can to foster that unity.[69]

Simply expressed, this was prophetic thinking, a Catholic taking responsibility for past divisions and future healing.

On another occasion Pawley asked Bea to clarify his reported statement in Switzerland that the 'Council was not primarily one for union'. He responded, with considerable insight, that the council was about the necessary preliminaries to union, in particular the matter of ecclesial authority which needs to be reviewed so as to be more acceptable to the Orthodox and the Protestants. Such was the lead that Bea offered the council in its first session, and Pawley was delighted.[70] The quality of Bea was again evidenced when non-Catholic Bishop de los Reyes, president of the National Council of Churches of the Philippines, mentioned in Rome that attempts he had made to liaise with Cardinal Rufino Santos of Manila gained little more than snubs and unkindnesses. Bea made up for it, the bishop remarking to Pawley that he is 'a man in whom is the spirit of Pope John – and I can't pay any warmer tribute than that'. John Moorman spoke of him as the 'kindly, affectionate, quiet, simple, elderly and holy man [who] came to be the symbol of the new

---

68 Pawley report 5: 1 May 1961.
69 Pawley report 24: 27 November 1961.
70 Pawley report 24: 27 November 1961.

spirit in the Church of Rome'.[71] Margaret Pawley, who was born in Germany, always enjoyed meeting Bea who had become a family friend; it also afforded her an opportunity to speak the language.

Willebrands was a man of wisdom and sensitivity. He was, for example, constantly concerned about how Pawley thought of the status afforded guests at the council; and to David Du Plessis, the South African-born Pentecostal, Willebrands said that 'the Pentecostals have an element to contribute to the life of the Church'.[72] This was also a prophetic statement.

Father Tom Stransky, an officer in the SPCU from 1960 to February 1970, regarded Pawley as a very sober man who enjoyed excellent relations with Paul VI and with many other people. Virginia Johnstone spoke of him as a great pioneer who made lots of friends. John Satterthwaite, who ran the ecumenical affairs office at Lambeth and also the council on Roman Catholic relations, did not share this positive assessment of Pawley. He thought Bernard was too open in his relations with Catholics, and sent many warning letters which made little or no impact on Bernard. A paper Pawley especially enjoyed was *Le Croix,* which published the forward thinking of the French *periti,* and since Satterthwaite controlled the purse strings he told Bernard he should not buy it but go to a library if he wished to read it.

English Catholicism Through Anglican Eyes

Monsignor Willebrands once expressed his opinion that religious hostility in England made Catholics 'more Roman' and Anglicans 'less Roman' than each would have been in a situation of understanding and peace. He added that there was no longer need for such a state of tension.

But old habits die slowly. Over a long history the Church of England developed as a national body with a character of

---

71 John Moorman, *Vatican Observed: An Anglican Impression of Vatican II*, London: Darton, Longman and Todd, 1967: 19.
72 Pawley report 25: 7 December 1961.

inclusiveness, over against the post-Reformation development of English Catholicism, identifiable as a mission arising out of a tradition of exclusiveness. One was strongly English and liberal in outlook, its identity enshrined in the laws of the land; the other was Roman and significantly Irish, suggesting a level of foreign control and a conservative outlook. Martyrs were made and enshrined, and inevitably identities were marked, not by any sense of communion, but by a strong and seemingly impenetrable barrier which was more than just religious.

In 1957 Herbert Waddams wrote a paper in which he attempted to identify the political and religious 'blocks' which kept Catholics and Anglicans apart. He noted among the English and the Scottish a deeply embedded suspicion of the Romans as being an alien race and an alien religion. They were mainly Irish and their representatives, especially among the religious orders, were largely foreign. Religiously, Catholics were brought up on the stories of the English martyrs 'so that their psychology is inimical to friendliness'.[73] Where Romans are in the majority, as is the case in several European countries, their attitude to religious liberty does not match the tolerance they claim when they are in the minority. The *raison d'être* of the Roman Church in England, he said, is to destroy the Church of England, undermining faith in it and in its sacraments. Their refusal to participate in common prayer is the ultimate block to any beginnings of an ecumenical relationship.

Waddams sought a remedy in dialogue. 'Dialogue must rest upon the common assumption that both parties are in some way bound to Christ, and that there is an area of agreement as Christians on which both may stand.'[74] Beyond dialogue,

---

73 Herbert M. Waddams, 'Possibilities of an Oecumenical dialogue in England – some random reflections,' 29.12. 1957, ibid. Harold Wilson, Labour Prime Minister in Britain, conveyed to Pope Paul VI in April 1975 'the understandable passions' the planned October canonization of Irishman Oliver Plunkett could arouse among Ulster Unionists and Loyalists, 'and engender a mood of triumphalism among Catholics'. '1975 canonisation alarmed Wilson' in *The Tablet* 7 January 2006: 31.
74 Ibid.

he called for common activity and common prayer. It was his Roman experience that he and Pope Paul were 'in some way bound to Christ'; he had yet to experience that commonality in England.

Bernard Pawley, though moulded in this world of Anglican–Catholic non-communion, had an added experience of Catholicism beyond the shores of Britain. He reflected on it in an article in the *Church Times* of June 1963:

> there are great winds of change blowing through the Roman Church . . . and the proponents of them were much stronger at high level than any of us had realized . . . as is well known, the Roman hierarchy (in England) is largely conservative, and so unrepresentative of the hierarchy throughout the world.[75]

Pawley observed – in October 1962 – that it would have been unthinkable a few years earlier for him, an Anglican, to be televised from the nave of St Peter's, amicably discussing conciliar issues with Cardinal Norman Gilroy of Sydney.[76] He was, however, equally aware of the presence and power of the Vatican diehards under the leadership of Cardinal Alfredo Ottaviani, and of the tension that could sometimes show itself in relations between various Vatican offices.

There was one exception with respect to the hierarchy in England. It was Christopher Butler, a convert from Anglicanism, abbot of Downside, and later an auxiliary bishop. For him the council was a second conversion. According to Hastings, he would 'now increasingly come forward as the one senior English voice, at once unimpeachably loyal to Rome, yet cognizant of the full weight of contemporary theological scholarship'.[77] A sampling of five other of England's Catholic hierarchy confirms Pawley's judgement, and for that matter the view of Hastings, too.

---

75 Pawley, article for *Church Times*: 14 June 1963.
76 Pawley report 49: 15 October 1962.
77 Adrian Hastings, *A History of English Christianity 1920–1985*, London: Collins, 1986: 565.

'One of the least co-operative' of the English hierarchy, Pawley observed in 1962, was Bishop Cyril Conrad Cowderoy of Southwark who refused to give Bernard his title, referring to him as 'Mr Pawley'. Pawley was not above a little retaliation. Aware that Paul VI and Mervyn Stockwood, Cowderoy's Anglican counterpart in Southwark, were friends and exchanged Christmas cards, Pawley sought a private papal audience for Stockwood which, he judged, should serve to 'wear down the aloofness' of Cowderoy.[78]

Bishop George Andrew Beck of Salford, when preaching in Westminster, expressed the opinion that if the English read history, they would become Catholics.[79] Following one of his conciliar interventions in 1963, Pawley was moved to write: 'It is amazing how English Roman Catholic bishops seem to interpret their ecumenical role as being the reiteration at every possible opportunity of those particular doctrines which provoke separation.' Pawley probably had in mind Beck's letter to *The Times* in 1949, explaining that he could not say the Lord's Prayer with an Anglican because when Catholics say 'Thy Kingdom come' they are praying for the conversion of all to Catholicism, an intention in which Anglicans obviously could not join. He also refused to give a joint blessing with the Bishop of Winchester on the grounds that the Bishop did not have valid orders and was 'only a layman'. [80]

Pawley was no great admirer of Cardinal William Godfrey of Westminster. He was formerly rector of the Venerable English College in Rome, and a senior student there made an April 1931 diary entry[81] that the 'Rector put up a notice about Protestant Bibles. No one should buy or retain same in the College. All

---

78 Pawley report 27: 27 February 1962.
79 Pawley report 34: 12 March 1962. Beck later became archbishop of Liverpool.
80 Christina Scott, 'A Historian and his World: A Life of Christopher Dawson', in Peter Hebblethwaite, *In the Vatican*, Bethesda: Adler and Adler, 1986: 147.
81 Adrian Hastings, *A History of English Christianity 1920–1985*, London: Collins, 1986: 274–5, 479.

centres of Protestant propaganda in Rome must be avoided.' In 1938 Godfrey was appointed Britain's first Apostolic Delegate, and eventually Archbishop of Westminster. According to Adrian Hastings he transformed the 'English hierarchy into a Roman clique'.

On 29 September 1961 Willebrands spent a day with Pawley in Ely, England, one point of the conversation being the need of Willebrands to 'interview Monsignor Derek Worlock who needed further conversion'.[82] Worlock was secretary to Cardinal Godfrey of Westminster and, as the council progressed, secretary in effect to the whole English group of bishops in Rome. Worlock expressed alarm that a complete set of the volumes of the bishops' replies from around the world was handed by the SPCU to the Archbishop of Canterbury. 'If so, it is alarming to realize that the Anglicans in England now know what the Catholic bishops think about them.' In Vatican-circle discussions about appointments to commissions, Godfrey and Worlock were drawn into Archbishop Marcel Lefebvre's camp, indicating something of the strength of their right-wing leanings. Yet, on the death of Godfrey in January 1963, Worlock is said to have warmed 'by a minute fraction of a degree as each week passed'. He became a convert to the cause of Christian unity which, for so long, he had disdained. Was it grace at work in his life, or ecclesiastical opportunism?[83] Incidentally, Worlock did not approve of Pawley, remarking that 'Canon Pawley still preserves a face like a boot and it is hard to understand how frequent reference is made to his great charm'.[84]

Cardinal Heenan, Archbishop of Westminster

Before considering the fifth and final in the selection of English Catholic bishops, it is pertinent to briefly refer to Archbishop Michael Ramsey's appointment to Canterbury in 1961, a post

---

82 Pawley report 16: 29 September 1961.
83 Clifford Longley, *The Worlock Archive*, London & New York: Geoffrey Chapman, 2000: 48–52.
84 Longley: 96.

he filled until 1974. Hebblethwaite considered that Ramsey was closer theologically to Rome than all his predecessors, yet he kept getting cold feet. Owen Chadwick confirms this thinking when he refers to two Lambeth staff in 1965 remarking that the Anglo-Catholic Ramsey was less enthusiastic about relations with Rome than was Fisher. Yet on 23 March 1966 the Archbishop met the Pope, and it is said that 'Archbishop Ramsey formed more than a respect, he formed an affection for Pope Paul'.[85]

In anticipation of Michael Ramsey's enthronement as Archbishop of Canterbury on 27 July 1961 Archbishop Heenan wrote from Liverpool to Cardinal Willebrands. The burden of his message was that the time was not yet ripe for accepting an invitation for a Catholic representation at the enthronement 'without risking a scandal'. Such an initiative tends to confirm Purdy's opinion that Heenan was not particularly attracted to Anglicans,[86] or perhaps that he did not really understand, nor had he come to terms with, 'non-Catholics' of any denomination. When on the subject of mixed marriages, for instance, he was decidedly unecumenical, describing non-Catholics in England as 'so-called church-going Protestants'.

Heenan's nomination as Archbishop of Westminster in September 1963 prompted Pawley to caution that he will need watching. And Pawley was ever watchful. As early as Heenan's enthronement Pawley wrote 'I am amused by his conception of "building a bridge to Lambeth," and hope it will be made wide enough for two-way traffic'.[87]

The problem, according to Hastings, was that Heenan was unsure which side he was on:

Theologically he was a pure conservative ultramontane, never questioning the theology he had learnt in Rome . . .

---

85 Owen Chadwick, *Michael Ramsey: A Life*, Oxford: Clarendon Press, 1990: 321.
86 Purdy: 40.
87 Pawley report 81: 30 September 1963.

His reformism could be vigorous but it derived from pastoral pragmatism and a warm, generous stream in his heart, not from any personal questioning of the absolute rightness of the Roman Catholic system he had been brought up in.[88]

His insecurity revealed itself most tellingly at the council, and Pawley was astute enough to pick it up. In the debate on the Church, Heenan said that he found paragraph 9 defective because it did not sufficiently emphasize the duty of preaching to non-Catholics to bring them into the Catholic fold – i.e. conversion. In September 1964 Pawley found Heenan's speech on the sixteenth-century Protestant–Catholic feud in England as 'contentious, inaccurate and provocative', in total contradistinction to the spirit of Paul VI, who said: 'In this great cauldron of human history many severe things were done of which we are all together culpable.' Eamon Duffy assessed Heenan as a gifted and charismatic pastor, but one 'who was temperamentally and intellectually ill-equipped to steer the community through the theological white water of the seventies'.[89]

It was in the debate on the Church in the Modern World that Heenan hit rock bottom. His speech on 28 October 1964 'was a brick of the first order and was taken very badly by the council'. He attacked the *periti,* accusing them of 'caring nothing for the ordinary teaching of bishops', nor even for that of the Pope. These remarks, aimed particularly at moral theologian Bernard Haering, generated some mirth, in the first instance that Heenan was chasing a 'red Haering and the other that he had had an attack of peritinitis'.[90]

Pawley delighted in a speech the day following from Abbot Benedikt Reetz, Superior-General of the Benedictines of Beuron. Having heard from Heenan that monks could not be expected to know anything about the world, the abbot admitted that he rose to speak in fear and trembling. He observed that the 40

---

88 Hastings: 564.
89 Ibid: 53.
90 Pawley report 150: 23 October 1964.

monks sent to England by Gregory the Great at the beginning of the seventh century must have seen their mission in terms of making angels out of angles, since they were not equipped to deal with the world.[91]

Pawley felt that Heenan did not emerge well from the council. He also feared that Heenan was determined to bring all ecumenical discussion in Britain under the control of the hierarchy, out of the hands of the religious orders 'who have so far been almost the only people who have anything to say to us'. He advised Canterbury to be equally determined to retain the freedom 'to discuss these matters where and with whom we choose'. He had in mind the freedom to deal directly with Rome and with religious orders in England. On Heenan's death in 1975, the Rector of the Venerable English College reminded his listeners at a Requiem Mass that the Cardinal 'had much to suffer, not least the pain of being misunderstood'.[92]

Pawley's view of 'Roman propaganda'

Occasionally Pawley's suspicion about things Catholic in England infected his otherwise warm and sympathetic views of the Church in Rome and the progress of the council. He could make sweeping statements which were decidedly unecumenical, and of questionable worth. While in Greece in October 1962, he warned suffragan Bishop Penteleimon of Achaia, of Rome's intended 'conversion' of Greece. To Pawley's disappointment there was hardly a reaction, which prompted Bernard to write: 'He seemed to me to be alarmingly complacent about the issue.'[93]

Roman 'propaganda' at times rendered Pawley almost paranoid.[94] In 1961 he spoke of an immense blast of propaganda about the Council in England, adding that the Church of England ought to answer. Less than a year on he did a

---

91 Pawley report 151: 27 October 1964.
92 Homily at San Silvestro, 19 November 1975, by Monsignor Murphy-O'Connor, *Venerabile*, 1978: 66.
93 Pawley report 47: 2 October 1962.
94 Pawley report 25: 7 December 1961.

most uncharacteristic thing, criticizing Cardinal Bea whom he sincerely admired and respected. The Cardinal, while in England, made two TV films which Pawley judged to be 'part of the carefully arranged propaganda being staged by the Romans as a build-up for the Council. Are steps being taken to see that they don't have the field to themselves?'[95] Then he became angry at the English press, in particular the *Sunday Times* of 24 November 1963, for referring to Cardinal Bernard Griffin as the Archbishop of Westminster, but Dr Stopforth as the Anglican Bishop of London. 'Are we drawing attention to this form of propaganda?'[96] In early 1964 he spoke, totally uncharacteristically of a dear friend – Paul VI's pilgrimage to the Holy Land as 'an occasion of much propaganda by Roman sources'.

What inflamed him more than anything was the likely canonization of the Forty English Reformation martyrs, Pawley interpreting it as yet another piece of 'anti-Anglican propaganda'. In the early sixties he sent off a four-page memo to Willebrands, which included a number of lines like 'It was as political spies first and not only as Roman priests that they were executed'.[97] The severity of his reaction alongside the more ecumenical opposition to the canonization by Bea and Willebrands stirred Heenan and quite a few other English bishops to work even more energetically for the canonization. The event took place in 1970 and without the kind of reaction that Pawley had predicted. Paul VI, in masterly fashion, turned what was being interpreted as a sectarian occasion into a truly ecumenical moment for Anglicans and Catholics: 'May the blood of these martyrs,' he said, 'heal the great wound inflicted on God's Church by reason of the separation of the Anglican Church from the Catholic Church . . . Their devotion to their country gives us the assurance that on that day when – God willing – the unity of faith and life is restored, no offence will be inflicted on the honour and integrity of a great country such as England.'

---

95 Pawley report 46: 31 August 1962.
96 Pawley report 106: 26 November 1963 which quotes from the *Sunday Times*, 24 November: 17.
97 Purdy: 40.

Late on the night before the ceremony, Paul VI added a sentence, written in his own hand:

There will be no seeking to lessen the legitimate prestige and usage proper to the Anglican Church when the Roman Church – this humble 'Servant of the servants of God' – is able to embrace her ever-beloved Sister in the one authentic communion of the family of Christ: a communion of origin and faith, a communion of priesthood and rule, a communion of saints in the freedom and love of the spirit of Jesus.[98]

The words chosen by Paul VI were an application of the formula of Dom Lambert Beauduin: 'The Anglican Church united but not absorbed'. The Archbishop of Canterbury took up this very idea when sending his Christmas greetings to the Pope on 15 December 1970:

I read with happiness the words Your Holiness spoke of warm and friendly feelings towards the Anglican Communion on the occasion of the Canonization of the Forty Martyrs. You can be sure that your warmth of feeling to us Anglicans is reciprocated . . . in the hope that one day there will be between us a consummated unity which conserves all that has been true and good in our several traditions during the days of our separation.

Death of John XXIII and Election of Paul VI

In May of 1963 it was confirmed that John XXIII was gravely ill with cancer of the stomach and the prostate. He died a month later, on 3 June. The favourite to succeed John XXIII was Montini, though Pawley reported that his 'left wing sympathies are said by some to tell against him'. Then came Monsignor Amleto Tondini's conclave oration which was 'heavily dosed

---

98 *Insegnamenti*, 1970: 1067.

with rightest sentiments', inviting the separated brethren 'being desirous to provide more securely for their eternal salvation, to return to the Church of Christ. One is conscious here,' remarked Pawley, 'of a deliberate and arrogant return to an offensive type of pre-Roncalli Romanism. The whole oration caused a wave of irritation to sweep over the city . . . but its effect was to move waverers in the centre more to the left.' Such was his assessment of the scene.[99]

On 21 June 1963 it was with pounding heart that Bernard stood in St Peter's piazza awaiting the presentation of the newly-elected Pope. The 'arch-enemy' of the so-called left, Cardinal Ottaviani, was entrusted with the announcement that the new Pope was Cardinal Montini:

> I was naturally thinking of the thrilling time we had at Milan in 1955 with Montini and of how he had said that we should live to see considerable changes in Christian relations in our lifetime. I took a bottle of champagne to the Secretariat and we toasted Pope Paul VI and the cause of Christian union. The whole movement can be taken to be a certain sign that God's hand is guiding our brethren of the Roman Church to better things.[100]

To the amusement of many, at the coronation some days later, it was Cardinal Ottaviani who placed the tiara on the head of Pope Paul VI.

---

99 Pawley report 75: 21 June 1963.
100 Pawley report 76: 21 June 1963.

3

Observing the Second Vatican Council

Whatever one might think of Cardinal Ottaviani, he was consistent. Suspicious of the developing Catholic desire for better relations with other Christians, he was understandably against any official Catholic representation at World Council of Churches (WCC) meetings. This stance created a real difficulty in the way of appropriate exchanges between the two bodies. Ottaviani refused to accept the SPCU's plan to send observers to the WCC third General Assembly in New Delhi, 18 November–15 December 1961. Bea, President of the SPCU, stood his ground, informing the Pope of his firm position. Ottaviani compromised, but so did Bea. Five Catholic representatives could attend, but none of them would be members of the conciliar preparatory bodies.

The Bull *Humanae Salutis*, of 25 December 1961, convoked the Vatican Council for some time in 1962. John XXIII, speaking of other Christians, said 'that not a few have already promised to offer their prayers for its success, and that they hope to send representatives of their communities to follow its work at close quarters'.[101] Again, despite Ottaviani's strictures, not only would there be Catholic representatives at the WCC, there would be observers from other Christian traditions at the Vatican Council.

---

101 John XXIII, *Humanae Salutis*, 25 December 1961, convoking the Second Vatican Council. Walter M. Abbott SJ, ed., *The Documents of Vatican II*, London: Geoffrey Chapman, 1966: 709.

The Council Observers

The Secretariat for Promoting Christian Unity (SPCU) was given responsibility for working on a programme for the observers, and for inviting them. Willebrands proposed admission of the observers to the general sessions, though they would not have the right to vote or speak. The SPCU would organize meetings to explain conciliar developments to them and to hear their reactions. These meetings would prove invaluable for both parties, as subsequent reporting will show.

Willebrands's initial idea was to invite experts on ecumenism from the various Christian communities rather than bishops or heads of communions. He soon realized the wisdom of leaving it to the invited churches to decide on who would be their representatives.

The year 1962 was an especially busy one for Willebrands. He made several journeys in an effort to courteously extend the invitations. The ancient Oriental or Chalcedonian churches all answered in the affirmative, but difficulties lay in the path of trying to extend invitations appropriately to the Orthodox. The first difficulty arose in Rome, where sensitivities existed in the SPCU's relationship with the Commission for the Oriental Churches. John XXIII decided to simplify matters, placing the SPCU in charge of all ecumenical concerns and conversations, thus eliminating those who had vested interests.

Willebrands made at least two visits to Patriarch Athenagoras, extending invitations to both the Greeks and the Russians through Constantinople. Therein lay his mistake, Moscow's *non possumus* being an indicator of the tension between Moscow and Constantinople, rather than as a negative to Rome.

Aware of the Orthodox tension, Willebrands then made a secret visit to Moscow, carrying an invitation to the Orthodox to send observers to the Council. The response was the arrival in Rome of two Russian delegates, Fathers Borovoi and Kotliarof, the day after the council began. Meantime, Athenagoras never received his expected reply from Moscow, believing in good faith that the Russians were not sending observers and that he should demonstrate solidarity with them, by not sending observers.

Of all the Protestant communities invited, only the Baptist World Alliance declined, though Dr Joseph H. Jackson, head of the National Baptist Convention, disassociated himself from the Alliance's decision, attending as a 'guest'. There were distinguished scholars, including Professor Kristen Skydsgaard, a Lutheran from Denmark and a member of Faith and Order, Professor Edmund Schlink from Germany, Professor Oscar Cullmann, a Lutheran New Testament scholar from Strasbourg and Paris, Dr Lukas Vischer from the WCC and pastor of the Reformed Church of Switzerland, and two Methodist representatives, Dr Harold Roberts from England and Professor Albert Outler from Texas.

Willebrands made a personal visit to the Archbishop of Canterbury to invite the Anglican observers. A ready and positive response was given. The leader appointed was the Right Revd John Richard Moorman, Bishop of Ripon in England, who would prove to be one of the principal ecumenical bridge-builders over the next 20 years. He was accompanied by the Revd Dr Frederick C. Grant of PECUSA,[102] retired professor of the New Testament at Union Theological Seminary, and Dr Charles Harold de Sousa, Archdeacon of Colombo, India. A further member, as a guest of the SPCU, was Canon Bernard Pawley, and later, Canon John Findlow, Pawley's successor as personal representative in Rome of the Archbishops of Canterbury and York. There were substitutes over the various sessions of the council, often enough, by competent theologians. These included Bishop Cuba'in of Lebanon, Father Ernest John

---

102 By official actions of 1783 and 1789 the Anglican Church in the USA was officially designated as the Protestant Episcopal Church. A number of attempts were made to drop the word 'Protestant' as no longer indicating who they had become. Finally, in 1967 the General Convention voted to add a preamble to the Constitution, describing the Church as '*The Protestant Episcopal Church in the United States of America,* otherwise known as *The Episcopal Church*'. The official page of the 1979 Book of Common Prayer says it is 'according to the use of *The Episcopal Church*'. Hence, there are three sets of unofficial initials: *PECUSA, ECUSA* (the most commonly used since 1967) and *TEC*.

of the Brotherhood of the Ascension in Delhi, Professor William Wolf, Eugene Fairweather and Massey Shepherd from the USA, and Canon Welsh of the College of Preachers at Washington, Dr Peter Day and Mr John Lawrence.[103] Howard Root was an alternate observer at the second session for the Bishop of Ripon when the latter was required to be in England. Howard was also present for the third and fourth sessions.

First gatherings of observers

On 11 October 1962 the first group of 38 observers from 17 churches, ecclesial communities and federations, and their translators, assembled in the tribune of St Longinus – very close to the main altar in St Peter's. This 'motley crew', as Pawley described them, comprised mainly Germans, British and Americans, with almost no Africans or Asians. About 18 months later a Baptist minister remarked that by then they regretted the absence of a Baptist presence at the council.

That same day – 11 October – Bernard Pawley suggested that the observers organize themselves as a group, agreeing to meet regularly. On Monday and Friday some of them prayed together in the Methodist Chapel, near Ponte Sant'Angelo.[104] Schlink, the German evangelist, succeeded in getting the group to accept a common spokesman, despite opposition from Moorman. On the second day of the council they were all received in private audience by the Pope.

A very close relationship developed between the observers and the SPCU. The observers were given copies of all documents,

---

103 John Moorman, *Vatican Observed*, London: Darton, Longman and Todd, 1967: 17–18.
104 The Church occupies a thirteenth-century building, formerly the property of the Friars of St Celsus. It was opened on 18 March 1877 as an Evangelical Free Church when Garibaldi's chaplain, Alessandro Gavazzi, preached the occasional sermon. In 1894 a bust of Gavazzi was erected on the Janiculum Hill. Since 1955 the church has been used by the English language Methodist congregation of Rome and by visiting Protestants.

including confidential papers, and they had Tuesday meetings with the SPCU staff to discuss matters debated in the *aula*. These meetings were first held in the Hotel Columbus, but as observer numbers grew they transferred to the *Foyer Unitas* in Piazza Navona, under the care of the Ladies of Bethany and the Franciscan Friars of the Atonement. As time passed the observers and the council fathers became more at ease with one another, especially over free cups of coffee and non-alcoholic drinks in the 'Bar Jonas' or the 'Bar Abbas', situated on either side of the nave of St Peter's. Near the sacristy stronger drinks were available at moderate prices where 'the Anglo-Saxon clergy in particular were regular clients'.[105]

The observers were not invited to speak in the *aula*, though they saw themselves as leading actors in a Catholic transition. Cardinal Bea realized that the bishops of the council, through the presence of the observers, were gradually being introduced to a new understanding of the fundamental ecumenical problem. Beyond the council, Catholics and other Christians were being offered a 'first' opportunity to come face to face with the reality of Christian division, and the possibility of healing.[106]

Interestingly, Moorman interpreted the presence of the observers at the council as both a check on any tendency to overly 'Romanize' the Church of Christ, and as a reminder to the Catholic Church that the rest of the Christian world also reflects on important issues.

John Richard Humpidge Moorman

Bishop Moorman (1905–89) was present for the duration of the Vatican Council, where not only his ease with Latin and Italian but also his vast knowledge of Christian history stood him in good stead. As a deeply committed Anglican he made an invaluable contribution to the observer meetings.

---

105 Patrick Smith, *A Desk in Rome*, London: Collins, 1974: 192.
106 Augustin Cardinal Bea, *The Way to Unity after the Council*, London: Geoffrey Chapman, 1967: 9.

Born in Leeds, he was brought up in an evangelical home where he was early exposed to the life of Francis of Assisi, who became his lifelong interest. John made almost annual visits to Franciscan places, lecturing frequently on Franciscan history and spirituality. He was regarded as a worldwide expert on the subject. While he was principal of Chichester Theological College and Chancellor of the cathedral there, he published the best-known of his 15 books: *A History of the Church in England,* a text which contributed significantly to an understanding of Anglicanism. John had great respect for George Bell whom he described as 'a truly catholic bishop', and it was George's episcopal ring, given him by Hetty Bell, that he wore when he became Bishop of Ripon in 1959.

He was prominent in ARCIC, 1969–81. In the debate on the ordination of women he was concerned that a unilateral move on the part of the Church of England would create new barriers and harm the progress already made in the dialogues with Rome and Constantinople.

As John reflected on his Christian life from its evangelical beginnings, he discovered an ever-deepening interest in the nature of the Church. He detected a personal change, more or less paralleling the development in the Church's self-understanding as expressed in the evolution of *Lumen Gentium*. The chapel of unity in Ripon Cathedral is fittingly restored in his memory.

First Council Session: 11 October–8 December 1962

In early October 1962 Cardinal Bea hosted a social for the observers and their wives and John XXIII met the observers in private audience. The next conciliar encounter for the observers was with the preparatory readings. These documents, provided by the Theological Commission, were something of an anti-climax. But the observers were not alone, for many of the council fathers and the vast majority of the *periti* had difficulty either digesting them or agreeing with their content. Relief it was when Cardinal Achille Liénart of Lille and Cardinal Josef Frings of Cologne moved that the personnel of the 16 pre-conciliar committees should not automatically continue in office. Elections were held and appropriate changes made.[107]

Four areas of interest to the observers in this first session were the liturgy, the sources of revelation, the unity of the Church and, finally, the schema on the Church. The proposals on the liturgy saw considerable agreement among many of the council fathers and the Anglican observers that the Mass and the breviary both badly needed reform, and that the vernacular should be introduced, though according to an acceptable expression of the English language. Not long into the session 'Cardinal Godfrey, conscious perhaps of the Anglican Church in his own country, felt that the introduction of communion under both kinds might give the impression that the Church had been mistaken in the past'.[108] It would take a while for the English Catholic hierarchy to become comfortable with an Anglican presence at the council. The liturgy scheme was referred to its commission for amendment and a later vote, as would happen to all the conciliar documents. The Constitution on the Sacred Liturgy *(Sacrosanctum Concilium)* was the first document to be promulgated, on 4 December 1963, John Moorman writing approvingly of the reform,[109] and Pawley commenting that it 'represents a considerable move forward, not only in matter but also in underlying theology'.

The debate on the sources of revelation brought many observers alive, as well as the council fathers. It was Bishop Emil de Smedt of Bruges who spoke for the SPCU, making the point that the document failed in the matter of unity. There was need of a new method 'free from any suggestion of opposition or urge for conversions'. He finished with a most moving peroration, saying that the schema was a retrograde step at the very point where

---

107 Pawley report 49: 15 October 1962.
108 Mathijs Lamberigts, 'The Liturgy Debate' in *History of Vatican II*. Giuseppe Alberigo and Joseph A. Komonchak, eds, Vol. II. 'The Formation of the Council's Identity. First Period and Intersession. October 1962–September 1963.' Orbis Maryknoll: Peeters Leuven, 1997: 129.
109 John Moorman: 46–8.

progress really could be made – not in union, but in the possibility of dialogue – now and in the future. Close the doors, he said, and the Second Vatican Council would be responsible for a very great mistake. Ottaviani did not hear the round of applause that followed, having absented himself from the council *aula* during the speech. The vote of about 1300 in favour of abandoning the schema, with about 800 in favour of continuing, was insufficient in a doctrinal matter, since a two-thirds majority was required. The decision was set aside, though the next day John XXIII intervened, directing that discussion cease and that the schema be recast under the joint chairmanship of Ottaviani and Bea.[110] Absent from the *aula* for two years, it was largely rewritten, emerging on 18 November 1965 as the Dogmatic Constitution on Divine Revelation (*Dei Verbum*), one of the two most fundamental documents of the council. Despite the improvements, Frederick C. Grant, writing two years after the ending of the council, said that 'the decree can only be temporary . . . There is so much to the Bible and its use. Catholic biblical studies are just beginning, and there is much yet to learn.'[111] He was right. The Vatican Council was not an ending, but the beginning of a movement. One very significant aspect of that movement is biblical studies, now undertaken collaboratively by scholars of many traditions.

The third document, from the preparatory committee of the Eastern Churches, was called 'The Unity of the Church: that all may be one'. It made no mention of the churches of the West, simply proposing uniatism as a model of reunion for the east. It was judged inadequate and was fittingly punished, both by the observers in their session and even more emphatically on the council floor. The debate lasted just three days, only 36 voting in favour. This document happened to be one of three 'unity' statements; eventually two of them would die a death, and the

---

110 Pawley report 59: 24 November 1962.
111 Frederick C. Grant, 'Divine Revelation' in *The Second Vatican Council: Studies by eight Anglican Observers*, Bernard C. Pawley, ed., London: Oxford University Press, 1967: 53.

SPCU would mastermind *Unitatis Redintegratio,* to which we will return later. Six days remained to consider the fourth document, the schema on the Church. That was more than enough time for a variety of speakers to rise and point to its inadequacies, including Cardinal Montini, who regarded it as out of touch, and in need of deep revision by both the Theological Commission and the SPCU. We will return to the evolution of *Lumen Gentium* later in this chapter.

Thus ended a stormy first session, effectively pointing to the inadequacies of the initial Theological Commission and demonstrating to the arch-conservatives that try as they might, their hold on the direction of the council and the Church was weakening. During this first session the total number of observers reached 54, including eight guests.[112] Moorman appraised these council beginnings quite positively: 'Whatever the outcome of the events, we must believe that honest and basic reforms are becoming inevitable for the Catholic Church.'[113]

In August 1963 several large confessional groups held their assemblies at a variety of locations around the world, all inviting Catholic observers. These included the Lutheran World Federation, the World Methodist Conference and the Anglican Assembly from 13 to 20 August, the first since 1954. Eighteen provinces were represented at the Anglican Assembly of over 1000 delegates, the theme being 'The Church's Mission in the World'. After it, Dr Ramsey said, 'the ultimate goal of the ecumenical movement was reunion with Rome, but, indeed, not with the Roman Church in its present form'.[114]

During the summer, before the beginning of the second session of the council, the SPCU produced a new schema of three chapters: (1) The Principles of Catholic Ecumenism; (2) The Implementation of Ecumenism; (3) Christians separated from the

---

112 Hilari Raguer, 'An Initial Profile of the Assembly' in *History of Vatican II*, Vol. II: 182. The figures they supply for each of the sessions are used in this text.
113 Jan Grootaers, 'Ebb and Flow Between Two Seasons' in *History of Vatican II*, Vol. II: 523.
114 Ibid: 540.

Catholic Church: I, the Oriental Orthodox Churches, II, Christian Communities arising after the sixteenth century. But on the presentation of the schema to the council in November 1963 two chapters had been added: (4) On the attitude of Catholics towards non-Christians, especially the Jews; and (5) 'Religious Liberty'.

Second Council Session: 29 September–4 December 1963

With the death of John XXIII on 3 June 1963 and the election of Giovanni Battista Montini on 21 June, a new spirit began to pervade the council. At the opening of the second session Paul VI spoke clearly and firmly, most especially on the subject of the Church, its place in the world and its relationships. Giving an example of proper relations, he addressed the 68 observers, including nine guests, as brothers, saying:

> If we are in any way to blame for that separation, we humbly beg God's forgiveness and ask pardon too of our brethren who feel themselves to have been injured by us. For our part, we willingly forgive the injuries which the Catholic Church has suffered.[115]

Still lurking, and intent on controlling the direction of the council, was Ottaviani. But he had to contend with Bea. The view of Clifford Longley is that the collision of Ottaviani and Bea was 'at the heart of the Second Vatican Council'. Ottaviani was not content with defending a position, he was intent on using the council to further his own reactionary agenda, the formation of an updated 'Syllabus of Errors'.[116] It was Ottaviani's Holy Office that requested the publisher of Congar's *True and False Reform in the Church* not to print a second edition. And this was done in the face of Pope Paul's recent remark that Congar was a

---

115 Quoted in Moorman: 68.
116 Clifford Longley, *The Worlock Archives*, London and NY: Geoffrey Chapman, 2000: 38.

theologian who had influenced him greatly.[117] Ottaviani[118] was aided by Tardini, the two of them viewed as curial and conciliar tyrants.

As the second session continued, Ottaviani and Tardini showed signs of being misunderstood and chastened. Now and then Ottaviani would reassert himself, though increasingly as a pathetic figure trying to ward off the episcopal hounds, as Pawley identified them. In November 1963, following Cardinal Frings's speech on collegiality, using impeccable and impromptu Latin, Ottaviani's defence of the Holy Office began *'altissime protestor . . .'*; the follow-up remarks heard in the *aula* were that Ottaviani had joined the Protestants![119] The emerging scene was of the bishops versus the curia in a big way, with Bea and his SPCU no longer obviously subjected to Ottaviani's tyranny. In their own right they were accepted as an increasingly significant presence in the life of the Church and the council.

The observers had a special interest in the twin subjects now before the assembly: 'Church' and 'ecumenism'. The first 23 days were given over to the subject of the Church and 11 days to ecumenism. The Anglicans were encouraged, albeit temporarily, by Archbishop Heenan's positive words in the debate on 20 November 1963. 'Some suspicious Catholics,' he said, 'eye the ecumenical movement with misgivings and would co-operate with other Christians only on the level of charity and sociology. This is not good enough.'[120] An interesting aside is that, out of the 163 bishops participating in the debate on ecumenism, it is reported that just two came from England: George Dwyer, then Bishop of Leeds, Heenan the other. It was a Frenchman, Bishop

---

117 Pawley report 107: 28 November 1963.
118 Cardinal Ottaviani, president of the preparatory theological commission of the council, and its secretary, Fr Sebastian Tromp, exercised immense controls over the members and subject-matter of the commission. Yves Congar, a member since July 1960 to the opening of the council on 11 October 1962, 'felt isolated within the commission'. See William Henn, 'Yves Congar and *Lumen Gentium*' in *Gregorianum* 86, 3, 2005: 565.
119 Pawley report 99: 11 November 1963.
120 Pawley report 103: 20 November 1963.

Bernadin Collin of Digne, who requested special treatment of the Anglican Communion.[121] Significantly more active than the English bishops, the observers helped shape the Catholic mind on ecclesiology and ecumenism.

Two schools of thought were evident among the observers. One school, including Professor Edmund Schlink, a German Lutheran, said that unless there was some real 'give' in the Catholic doctrinal position, for instance on infallibility, any future dialogue was useless. These people, Pawley sensed, and he is expressive of the second school of thought,

> seem to want the Pope more or less to become Lutheran before they will start real discussion. They never give any indication of a willingness to come out from inside their own doctrinal stockade. We do not hold this firm line, in fact we have to conceal our haste to throw the 39 Articles into some good ecumenical melting pot.[122]

Pawley was of a mind that the 1963 draft on ecumenism was the result of a long struggle and represented an optimum of what could be expected.[123] Nikos Nissiotis, still dissatisfied with the document, asked what was its purpose, giving it the title, 'the Catholic view of Ecumenism'.[124] It would be a waste of time, he emphasized, to expect the Orthodox to consider reunion with Rome if obliged to accept Latin discipline. In the face of such negativity on the part of his fellow-observers, Pawley often rose in defence of the council efforts, saying 'We have to be careful that the hoped-for dialogue is not closed before it begins.'[125]

The observers were particularly keen to detect what was the

---

121 Xavier Rynne, *Vatican Council II*, New York: Orbis, 1999: 254.
122 Pawley report 106: 26 November 1963.
123 Pawley report 101: 14 November 1963.
124 Pawley report 107: 28 November 1963.
125 See Howard Root, *The Search for Unity: Relations Between the Anglican and Roman Catholic Churches From the 1950's to the 1970's*, London: Geoffrey Chapman, 1966: 70–3 for a consideration of the Anglican response to the 1963 draft schema, and a comparison with some Protestant responses.

conciliar thinking on the People of God. It was one thing for individual baptized Christians to be thought of as incorporated into the Church, but what about their communities? Day by day the Catholic conception of the Church broadened, the observers making significant contributions to it. The presence of the observers, according to B. Olivier, as 'a silent but close presence, is exercising a great influence on the debates. Each father who speaks is conscious of speaking in their presence, and many speak for them.'[126] On 15 October 1963, for instance, Cardinal Albert Meyer made his own on the council floor the remarks of Lutheran Professor Skydsgaard. People such as Dr Lukas Vischer of the WCC, George Lindbeck of the Lutheran World Federation and H. Roux of the World Alliance of Reformed Churches, and the Anglican group, were asking basic questions about how the Catholic Church visualized itself in relation to other Churches. It became obvious that the council was groping, not only for the right words, but for the right ideas. Schlink spoke forcefully on the subject at the observers' meeting, saying that the 'Roman Church still seems intent on treating non-Catholics wholly as individuals'.[127] The Abbot of Downside, Dom Christopher Butler, speaking in the *aula* the very next day, reflected something of the new Catholic self-understanding, and the emerging understanding that non-Catholic communions, 'though imperfect from a Catholic stand point, Churches they are'.

There was widespread disquiet among the observers on the two additional chapters of the ecumenism document. While the Anglican group and Lukas Vischer approved of the letter and spirit of the chapter on the Jews, they eventually joined five other observers who thought its proper place was not in a

---

126 Giuseppe Ruggieri, 'Beyond an Ecclesiology of Polemics. The Debate on the Church' in *History of Vatican II*, Vol. II: 290, footnote 126.
127 Pawley report 106: 26 November 1963.

decree on ecumenism.[128] A consistent Anglican view was that 'interreligious' concerns did not fall under the umbrella of 'ecumenism', an added danger being that the Catholic under-standing of ecumenism would be seen as little more than a gesture of benevolence to all people of goodwill.[129] Both in the *aula* and in the observers' meetings there was an aware-ness of Jewish thought that a level of anti-semitism existed, and among the Arabs a sense that the wording of the schema could be interpreted as support for the state of Israel. The outcome was the removal of the chapter from the ecumenism document and the creation of a new one, the Declaration on the Relation-ship of the Church to Non-Christian Religions (*Nostra Aetate*), promulgated on 28 October 1965. In the judgement of John Moorman it was 'a rather feeble document'.[130] Chapter 5 on Religious Freedom would also become a separate document, the Declaration on Religious Freedom (*Dignitatis Humanae*) which we shall return to later. In the opinion of Pawley, after the struggle about Mary, the second most painful subject was that of religious freedom. Strongly opposed by the prelates of the so-called 'Catholic countries', Ottaviani spoke on their behalf in opposition to it, delivering it 'with a consummate oratory. He is the only speaker who *really* speaks Latin.'[131] It was even-tually passed, but not until 7 December 1965.

The title change of the first chapter of the scheme on ecu-menism from 'Principles of Catholic Ecumenism' to 'Catholic Principles of Ecumenism', revealed something of the nature of the change that was occurring in the council. According to Walter Abbott:

---

128 Claude Soetens, 'The Ecumenical Commitment of the Catholic Church' in *History of Vatican II*, Giuseppe Alberigo and Joseph Komonchak, eds, Vol. III. 'The Mature Council. Second Period and Intersession. September 1963–September 1964'. Orbis Maryknoll: Peeters Leuven, 2000: 292–3.
129 See Howard Root, 'The Church and Non-Christian Religions' in *The Second Vatican Council: Studies by eight Anglican Observers*, Bernard C. Pawley, ed., London: Oxford University Press, 1967: 235.
130 J. Moorman, *Vatican Observed*: 127.
131 Pawley report 133: 25 September 1964.

The change implies that the Council recognizes ecumenism as one movement for all Christian Churches and Communities. The goal for all is the same, unity in the Christian faith, but the way of conceiving that unity and faith may vary, and so one may speak of a Church having its own principles of ecumenism.[132]

During the debates on the Church and ecumenism there was an ever-growing confidence in relations between the observers and the council fathers. There was the occasional 'hiccup' which created some strains. One occurred on 23 October at the beatification of the Passionist, Dominic Barberi, whom Paul VI praised for his part in the 'conversion' of John Henry Newman from Anglicanism to Catholicism.[133] Another was on 25 November 1963 when there was a ceremonial transfer of the relics of St Josaphat Kuncewicz, a great promoter of the union of the Ukrainians with Rome at the end of the sixteenth century, one whom the Orthodox held responsible for the martyrdom of certain Orthodox saints. The principal observer from the Patriarchate of Moscow, Archpriest V. Borovoy, received an order to leave Rome. In fact, he did not leave; he simply absented himself from St Peter's to attend a Requiem Mass elsewhere in Rome for President Kennedy on that same day.[134]

The morning of 3 December 1963 was given over to a commemoration in St Peter's of the 400th anniversary of the Council of Trent. Quite a few notable observers judged it better to absent themselves because Trent was 'more in the nature of a disaster to be mourned'. John Moorman, who was one of the few to attend, saw his role in Rome to observe and not to protest. Pawley absented himself to do paperwork, commenting that on 2 and 3 December 1564 the decrees on purgatory and

---

132 'Decree on Ecumenism' in *The Documents of Vatican II*, Walter M. Abbott SJ, ed., London: Geoffrey Chapman, 1966: footnote 9: 343.
133 Alberto Melloni, 'The Beginning of the Second Period: The Great Debate on the Church' in *History of Vatican II*, Vol. III: 94.
134 Claude Soetens, 'The Ecumenical Commitment of the Catholic Church': 294.

indulgences were rushed through, 'for which we give no thanks at all'.[135]

By now Paul VI had stopped saying that the 'next session' of the council will be the last. Cardinal Giuseppe Siri of Genoa, and of the extreme right wing, was emphatic that one more session was enough. Others were not quite so sure.

Third Council Session: 14 September–21 November 1964

The number of observers continued to increase session by session. For the third session 83 were in attendance, including 13 guests. For the first time representatives of the Patriarchate of Constantinople were present, seen by many as the fruit of Paul VI's meeting with Patriarch Athenagoras I in Jerusalem. Also for the first time, the Greek Orthodox Patriarchate of Alexandria was represented. Lukas Vischer spoke of the observers at this session as far less effective than they had been at the first two sessions. Their 'quality' was lower and their 'interests so varied' that it was 'difficult to form a common mind'.[136]

On 17 September the observers decided to form a small co-ordinating committee, comprising Professor Edmund Schlink, Father Vitaly Borovoy, Canon Bernard Pawley and Lukas Vischer. Weekly meetings with members of the SPCU continued, Vischer assessing them as not having the 'same impetus' because the SPCU was so busy. The general congregation on 23 September began with a veneration of the relics of St Andrew, before they were returned to Patras in Greece. While Cardinal Franz König called this act a sign of the desire and hope for unity, the Waldensian Vittorio Subilia, delegate of the World Presbyterian Alliance, wrote of it as 'a profanation and counterfeiting of ecumenism'.[137]

---

135 Pawley report 110: 4 December 1963.
136 *History of Vatican II*, Giuseppe Alberigo and Joseph A. Komonchak, eds, Vol. IV, 'Church as Communion: Third Period and Intersession. September 1964–September 1965', Orbis Maryknoll: Peeters Leuven, 2003: 17.
137 Ibid: 18.

Writing in May 1964 Pawley detected a definite maturing of the Catholic ecumenical mind. Whereas in 1962 the Catholic prayer for unity was for the *return* of the Orthodox, the Protestants and the Anglicans to the Catholic Church, a year later it was prayer for their *reconciliation* with the Holy See.[138] But in 1964 it was prayer *for* the Orthodox, the Anglicans and the Protestants. That same month, Robert McAfee Brown, an influential Presbyterian observer, offered an affirmation of the ecumenical document as it continued to evolve: 'We now know that ecumenism has definitely taken root in the Roman Church.'[139] In June Willebrands was nominated a titular bishop, which meant a seat in the council and an upgrading of the status of the SPCU.

WCC interest in the growing Catholic attention to ecumenism prompted a four-day consultation in July 1964 with some of the official Vatican II observers at Rummelsberg, near Nuremburg. A follow-up to this fruitful consultation would be the formation of a Joint WCC–RC Committee in 1965 where the problems of Christian unity could be addressed. Ten days after the ending of the Rummelsberg meeting, Paul VI produced his first encyclical, *Ecclesiam Suam* of 6 August 1964. It was judged by Moorman to be a disappointing document, a kind of old triumphalism revived, so different to Paul VI's remarks at the beginning of the second session in 1963.[140] It seemed to Moorman, as well as to some others, that Paul was falling under the influence of a small, though strong, conservative group. Xavier Rynne (Father Francis X. Murphy CSs R) considered the third session of the council 'the most disappointing of all'. As the council fathers returned, 'many of them wondered whether the Council was really going to succeed in its dual task of *aggiornamento* and *ecumenismo*'. Their reason for thinking this way, according to

---

138 Pawley report 122: 19 May 1964.
139 Pawley report 121: 13 May 1964.
140 Moorman's view on the encyclical is not shared, for example, by Alberigo and Komonchak. Cf *History of Vatican II*, Vol. III: 448ff and 509.

Pope Paul VI and Archbishop Michael Ramsey, with Bishop
John Moorman, centre, during the Archbishop's visit to the
Pope in March 1966.

Père Hamard and Monsignor Arrighi, members of the
Secretariat for promoting Christian Unity, and Frank Doria-
Pamphilj, owner of the Palazzo, home to the Anglican Centre
in Rome, at the opening of the Centre in October 1966.

Bishop Jan
Willebrands,
Secretary of the
Secretariat for
Promoting Christian
Unity, and Canon
John Findlow, 1966.

Canon Bernard
Pawley and his
wife Margaret,
1964.

Cardinal Bea, 1966.

Pope Paul VI, Archbishop Donald Coggan,
Cardinal Willebrands and Canon Dr Harry Smythe,
Director of the Anglican Centre, 1977.

Canon Howard Root and his wife Celia say goodbye to the
Pope at Castelgandolfo, September 1991.

Pope John Paul II and Father Douglas Brown SSM, with the
Revd Peter Marchant (centre), 1992.

Archbishop Robert Runcie attends Papal Mass with
Pope John Paul II, 1 October 1989.

The Archbishop George Carey blesses the new Centre, with left to right, Vivien Ruddock, Bishop Mark Santer, Chairman of the Governors, Canon Bruce Ruddock, Director of the Centre, Canon David Hamid, and Cardinal Cassidy, February 1999.

The entrance of the Anglican Centre in Rome in the Palazzo Doria Pamphilj, Piazza Collegio Romano.

HM Queen Elizabeth II greets Cardinal Cassidy, with Bishop
John Baycroft, during her visit to the Centre in October 2000.

Pope John Paul II with Bishop Richard Garrard and
Archbishop Carey.

Archbishop Rowan Williams greeting Pope John Paul II, October 2003.

Bishop John Flack and Mr Francis Campbell, Ambassador to the Holy See from December 2005

Archbishop
Williams and
Cardinal Walter
Kasper.

Pope Benedict XVI and Bishop John Flack, 2005.

Moorman, was because Pope Paul seemed so willing to go to any length to soothe the feelings and assuage the doubts of an organized group of bullies.[141] He was not entirely right.

An especially depressing few days was *la settimana nera,* the 'black week' of 14–21 November 1964 when a number of events caused dismay in the assembly. The first pertained to the document on religious liberty. On 19 November Bishop Emil de Smedt, a consummate orator, was greeted with great applause when he presented the report, revealing to the assembly how the printing had been deliberately held up and a variety of manoeuvres had delayed the document's arrival. The applause was most moving, the longest ever accorded a speaker in the entire council. Bishops stood and shouted, while the old Italian cardinals looked glum, according to Pawley. Though De Smedt did not agree with every aspect of the report, he was convinced that the vote should not be delayed.

Then came Cardinal Eugene Tisserant's announcement, in the name of the Pope, that the vote on Religious Liberty would be held over to the next session. This action prompted 456 Fathers to send a letter of protest to Paul VI. Its opening line said: 'Reverenter sed instanter, instantius, instantissime petimus . . .' (Respectfully but insistently, even more insistently, very instantly we request . . .)[142] These Fathers did not appreciate that the Pope was very interested in the subject of religious liberty and that he was favourably disposed to the report. Given the opposition, he had to choose a prudent path, delaying the vote until the next session.

The second trauma was the Pope's intervention on three occasions during the week, introducing a total of 19 alterations[143] to the *Decree on Ecumenism.* The text had already been voted

---

141 Moorman: 110.

142 Luis Antonio G. Tagle, 'The "Black Week" of Vatican II (November 14–21 1964)' in *History of Vatican II*, Vol. IV: 393.

143 These alterations or *modi* were originally more than 19, but the excess were rejected, with reasons given, by the Secretariat. It is also clear that the point of origin of many of the *modi* was not Paul VI, but C. Boyer and/or L. Ciappi.

on and approved by the assembly, and was destined for a final vote and promulgation before the end of the session. Congar became angry at the Pope's action, attributing it to his 'lack of a true theology of ecumenism',[144] but he calmed down on discovering that the changes had not altered the substance of the Decree. Moorman was quite dismayed, asking of Paul VI:

> Where does he stand? What is he really trying to do? How far is he in favor of reform, or how far is he falling into the clutches of the 'old guard' who are using all their skill and determination to stifle those movements which they can only see as threats to their own power?[145]

It is the opinion of Tagle that Paul VI had no intention of undermining the developing Catholic theology of ecumenism. The fact is that Paul, like so many of the council fathers, was going through the process of discovering a theology that was new to him. His position and his style combined to persuade him to act with the greatest caution.[146]

A third event was the Pope's closing speech of the session in which he proclaimed Mary Mother of the Church, a title which the doctrinal commission – for doctrinal, pastoral and ecumenical reasons – had deliberately omitted from the chapter on Mary in *Lumen Gentium*.[147] The commission was very much aware of the widespread concern among the observers, and a growing number of the council fathers, of the level of attention being given to Mary. Some council fathers hoped for a special document, while others looked for another Marian definition. Against this background Nissiotis, who Congar said 'is *absolutely not* a man for dialogue',[148] spoke at the meeting of observers, attributing this preoccupation to a lack of pneumatology in

---

144 Ibid: 412.
145 Ibid: 416 quoting Stransky: 'Paul VI and the Delegated Observers'.
146 Ibid: 415.
147 Luis Antonio G. Tagle, 'The "Black Week" of Vatican II (November 14–21 1964)' in *History of Vatican II*, Vol. IV: 395 and 448.
148 Giuseppe Alberigo, 'Major Results, Shadows of Uncertainty' in *History of Vatican II*, Vol. IV: 632, quoting Congar.

Catholicism, suggesting that much of what 'Father Benoit's exegesis attributed to Mary are the energies of the Holy Spirit'. Congar saw Father André Scrima, Patriarch Athenagoras' personal envoy, as offering a more balanced assessment at the same meeting. But Pawley saw Nissiotis's speech as epitomizing the work of the council at its best.[149] What prevailed in the end, by the narrowest of votes, was the decision not to speak of Mary separately, but in the document on the Church, *Lumen Gentium,* which in effect placed Mary in the Church, not over it. Yves Congar interpreted this move as a 'return-to-sources' Catholicism, replacing a Catholicism that ignored the sources. Butler suggested that devotion to Mary, therefore, would gain in quality, and relations with other Christians would be enhanced.[150] The result was judged a triumph for the moderates, but then Paul VI's last-minute intervention on 21 November 1964 meant that, in the words of Bernard Pawley, 'many of the Protestant observers left the Council totally disillusioned and dumbfounded after Paul's amazing blast of Mariology'.[151]

Other matters that gradually clarified were the sections in the ecumenical document on the Reformation and its consequences, and the differences between Anglicans and Protestants. Early on there was a tendency in the debates to bundle the two together, but then in the closing stages of the second session there was repeated mention of not allowing this to happen. Clearly the conciliar setting was increasingly a forum for clarifications of historical facts, and of theological education and development. In the draft presented at the session beginning in September 1964, and ultimately in the final document *Unitatis Redintegratio,* in terms of its relationship with the Catholic Church, 'the Anglican Communion occupies a special place'.[152] Just as there was a level of sympathy or understanding of Anglicanism in France

---

149 Pawley report 132: 23 September 1964.
150 Moorman: 74–5.
151 Pawley report 166: 25 November 1964.
152 No 13 in *Unitatis Redintegratio, The Documents of Vatican II,* Walter M. Abbott SJ, ed., London, Geoffrey Chapman: 356.

before the council, so now in the debate on the ecumenical document some French bishops lent their support. The only English speaker who favoured special mention of Anglicanism was Abbot Butler of Downside.[153]

In the closing weeks of 1964 when Pawley sensed that the promulgation of the Decree on Ecumenism was near, he became concerned that Anglicans 'be properly led' in responding to the document.

> It will not be difficult for ill-disposed Anglican prophets to show from the published documents that all the old barriers are still there, undestroyed, and so to evaluate the Council as a failure. Considerable effort should be made to show that not only do paper documents represent an immense advance in comparison with their predecessors but behind them lies the great struggle, which still goes on. Our friends in the Roman Church have won much ground, more than we thought they would, against a deep and sinister conspiracy of powerful, politically-minded reactionaries. Our understanding reception of the results of the Council will help our friends to continue the struggle.[154]

He was right, for on 21 November 1964 the Dogmatic Constitution on the Church *(Lumen Gentium)*, the Decree on Ecumenism *(Unitatis Redintegratio)* and the Decree on Eastern Catholic Churches *(Orientalium Ecclesiarum)* were voted on and solemnly promulgated by the Pope. 'This event,' in Pawley's estimation, was 'undoubtedly a milestone in Church history ... It confirms the picture we have constantly drawn (in season, out of season) of the present Pope as a friend in the long run of reform and enlightenment.' In Pawley's understanding Paul VI and the council are to be seen 'as progressive and a matter of thanksgiving'.[155] Cardinal Bea saw the vote of approval for the

---

153 Moorman: 99.
154 Pawley report 127: 8 September 1964.
155 Pawley report 166: 25 November 1964.

Decree on Ecumenism by 2137 votes and only 11 against as 'a result one would not have dared to dream of two years before . . . because most of the Council Fathers . . . had never before been brought face to face with Christianity's sad divisions, and so with the ecumenical problem'.[156]

The Pawley Farewell and the Findlow Arrival

Bernard Pawley was no stranger to the papal apartments, having had three audiences during the month of October. It was on the occasion of the third, which was private, that he advised Paul VI that he was to be replaced by John Findlow. The Pope asked his impressions of the council, Pawley suggesting a senate of bishops, noting the Pope's reaction: 'He smiled the smile he always smiles when he doesn't want to talk about something.'[157]

Bishop Willebrands, and the whole staff of the SPCU, hosted the Pawleys at a farewell dinner in the Columbus Hotel on 26 November 1964. Bishop Willebrands, in his farewell remarks said that the Anglicans tried to understand what was going on in the Catholic Church and to evaluate it pragmatically. It was a good assessment. Two days later Paul VI invited Bernard and Margaret and their two children, Felicity (3) and Matthew (2), to the Vatican. 'Our private talk,' Pawley wrote, 'offered opportunities for exchange at quite a deep level, without wasting time on courtesies.'[158]

Margaret Pawley measured the changing climate of ecumenism in Rome by the way the Vatican treated the wives of the observers. They were not invited to the opening session of the council, she said, probably due more to oversight than to any deliberate choice not to include them. Thereafter they were invited to all the public sessions, and to functions specially

---

156 Augustin Cardinal Bea, *The Way to Unity after the Council*, London: Geoffrey Chapman, 1967: 39.
157 Pawley report 142: 13 October 1964.
158 Pawley report 167: 30 December 1964.

intended for them. Monsignor Vodopevic looked after them with care and good humour, and on approaching St Peter's in their company on one occasion, he explained to the surprised Swiss Guards at the barriers that these ladies were *les dames des observateurs!* 'Our tickets read in Italian that we had personal permission to assist in the august presence of His Holiness the Pope, and this is how it felt. We had in some way played a part,' recalled Virginia Johnstone, Bernard Pawley's secretary. Not only did Virginia play her part in establishing the Anglican presence in Rome; she has remained a great supporter of the Anglican Centre. Fittingly, in 2005 she was awarded the Cross of St Augustine by Archbishop Williams for her work for the Centre and in other ecumenical activities.

John Findlow assumed the task of official representative of the Archbishop of Canterbury in Rome at the beginning of 1965. Born in Cheshire, Findlow was ordained in 1939. He became an expert on Orthodoxy, enjoying fluency in Russian, French, German and Italian. After serving as general secretary to the Council on Foreign Relations John first came on appointment to Rome in 1949 as chaplain to All Saints' in Via del Babuino, a post he filled for eight years. According to Satterthwaite it was here that John made a name for himself, his wife Irina also making a name for herself. 'She dressed flamboyantly and spoke bluntly. I was very fond of her,' he told me when I visited him in Carlisle in February 2003.

After four years in Switzerland, followed by a very satisfying number of years in Athens, the Findlows arrived in Rome again in January 1965 as the Archbishop's representative to the Vatican and as observer of the third session of Vatican II. The other part of his appointment was as secretary to the Archbishop's Commission on Roman Catholic relations at Lambeth. In his letter of acceptance he remarked that after a long spell, and a love of Orthodoxy and Greece, 'it is strange and not a little overwhelming to think of the Latin West Department in my hands'.[159]

The Findlows occupied the flat vacated by the Pawleys in St Paul's Within-the-Walls in Rome; in London they were provided

---

159 Irina Findlow, *Journey Into Unity*, London: New City, 1975: 89.

with a flat in one of the Towers at Lambeth. Virginia Johnstone remarked that 'they fitted less happily into the American atmosphere of St Paul's' but they helped Virginia see Rome from a new and more cosmopolitan angle. John's first official appointment was an audience with the Pope who was surprised at his fluent Italian. The fourth session of the council began on 14 September, and John took his place with the observers in the tribune of St Longinus.

Fourth Council Session: 14 September–8 December 1965

Four times in his opening address at the fourth session, Paul VI referred 'to this final session' of the council. He was expressing not only his own but the widely shared wish and hope of the council Fathers, the observers and *periti* for an ending to the long and sometimes tedious conciliar process. Eleven documents remained for debate and vote, in the presence of 106 observers, including 16 guests.

As Robert McAfee Brown said:

> It is symbolically important that the Pastoral Constitution on the Church in the Modern World and the Declaration on Religious Freedom were promulgated on the last working day of the council, so that the council concluded on a note of concern for others.[160]

The date was 7 December 1965. But the journey to this moment, with respect to both of these documents was a long and dreary one, even involving expressions of anger at times, especially in the ongoing debates on religious freedom, as we have already noted.

McAfee Brown judged the Constitution on the Church in the Modern World *(Gaudium et Spes)* as a valuable first word,

---

160 Dr Robert McAfee Brown, 'A Response: Pastoral Constitution on the Church in the Modern World', *The Documents of Vatican II*, Walter M. Abbott SJ, ed., London: Geoffrey Chapman, 1966: 310.

though certainly not a last word. That opinion was shared widely, with quite a number of the Fathers wondering why such a document was part of an ecumenical council.

In Pawley's opinion the Catholic Church should be more modest about itself; after all, in various parts of the world, particularly Italy, it had a very bad record, resisting new knowledge and social improvements. Findlow said the document was too wordy, quoting Cardinal Heenan who felt the first chapter should be dropped because 'it gave hardly any valuable guidance to married couples in their intimate problems'.[161] Findlow concluded: 'It can hardly be said that the Pastoral Constitution is a worthy companion for its dogmatic counterpart on the Church.'[162]

It was William J. Wolf's opinion that the Declaration on Religious Freedom 'is properly the presupposition to many of the other decrees and to the potential influence of them all'. In another sense the Declaration 'has simply brought the Roman Catholic Church to the point reached generations ago by the best secular thought and by most of the other churches'.[163] John Courtney Murray SJ, who masterminded the document, said as much:

> It can hardly be maintained that the Declaration is a milestone in human history – moral, political, or intellectual. The principle of religious freedom has long been recognized in constitutional law, to the point where even Marxist-Leninist political ideology is obliged to pay lip-service to it. In all honesty it must be admitted that the Church is late in acknowledging the validity of the principle.[164]

Consideration of the documents on priestly life, bishops, religious life and laity moved rather rapidly during this session. The first

---

161 *The Second Vatican Council: Studies by eight Anglican Observers*, Bernard C. Pawley, ed., *The Church in the Modern World*, Findlow: 219.
162 Anglican Observers, *The Church in the Modern World*, Findlow: 229.
163 Anglican Observers, *Religious Liberty*, William J. Wolf: 175.
164 Abbott: 673.

scheme on what was to become the Decree on the Ministry and Life of Priests (*Presbyterorum Ordinis*) was seen, not just by Moorman but by an increasing number of council fathers, as a totally inadequate set of ten propositions about priests as bishops' assistants. In its new form in 1965, together with an improved statement in the Decree on Priestly Formation (*Optatam Totius*), a more positive understanding was made of priests as sharing in the ministry of Christ as Teacher, Priest and King.

What eventually emerged as the Decree on the Appropriate Renewal of the Religious Life (*Perfectae Caritatis*) was judged by the observers in November 1964 as soulless and too juridical. But the 1965 revised text, according to Moorman, was a much more satisfactory document, 'far more worthy of a fine body of men and women, to whom everyone felt that justice had now been done'.[165] William A. Norgren, a priest of PECUSA and a guest of SPCU at the Council, said:

> If, as the Decree proposes, the adaptation, and renewal of Roman Catholic religious orders is centred in a constant return to the sources of all Christian life, the holy Scripture, and if Protestants, too, constantly return to the Gospels as they profess they do, monasticism may no longer be a bone of contention but a means to the recomposition of all Christians in unity.[166]

The 1964 debate on what was to become the Decree on the Apostolate of the Laity (*Apostolicam Actuositatem*) revealed that the laity had not been consulted. The document formally promulgated on 18 November 1965 is unlikely to stand out among the decrees which have done much to renew the life of the Church.[167]

An interesting observation about the quality of the council texts is that of Giuseppe Dossetti, theological adviser to Cardinal Giacomo Lercaro of Bologna, who 'regarded its final

---

165 Anglican Observers, *The Ministry*: Moorman: 107.
166 Abbott: 484–5.
167 Anglican Observers, *The Ministry*: Moorman: 111.

texts as greatly compromised by Paul VI's caution and his desire for near-unanimity'.[168] *Gaudium et Spes*, particularly, did not come anywhere near the level of evangelical radicalism that the world needed.

The council concludes

Three services in the early days of December brought the council to its end. The first of these was on 4 December, a joint service in St Paul's Outside-the-Walls. Dr Albert C. Outler, a Methodist, read an Old Testament lesson; Father Pierre Michalon, a successor of the Abbé Paul Couturier, read a passage from Romans; Archimandrite Maximos of the Greek Orthodox Church read the Beatitudes in Greek; hymns were sung in English. Canon Maan of the Old Catholic Church led the congregation in prayer, and Paul VI articulated quite sensitively and truthfully in French the nature of the bond that had built up among the observers, the *periti*, the bishops and the officials of the council:

> Dear Observers, or rather let us call you by the name which has sprung to life again during these four years of the Ecumenical Council: Brothers and Friends in Christ. Now the Council is drawing to its close and you are going to leave us; we wish, in this moment of farewell, to become the interpreter of the Venerable Council Fathers who have come with us this evening, to pray with you and to say good-bye.
>
> Each of you is going back to his own home, and we shall find ourselves alone. Let us share with you this deep impression: your departure will leave a loneliness around us which we knew nothing of before the Council but which now saddens us; we would like to see you among us always.
>
> This obliges us to say once again how grateful we are for your presence at our Ecumenical Council. We have greatly appreciated this presence; we have felt its influence; we have

---

168 Joseph Komonchak, 'What road to joy?' *The Tablet* 30 November 2002: 11–12.

admired its nobility, its piety, its patience, its friendliness. And that is why we shall keep a grateful memory of your coming.[169]

John Moorman replied on behalf of all the observers:

> The Council is drawing to its end; but the work for Christian Unity is but beginning. We outside the communion of the Roman Church have for long been occupied in prayer, in dialogue and in effort for the union of our respected Churches. Now, with the entry of the Roman Catholic Church into this field, we realize that the Ecumenical Movement has taken on a new dimension. At last we can say that the whole Christian world is engaged in the search for that unity for which Our Lord prayed.[170]

The second of the concluding services was also the last public session of the council at St Peter's, on 7 December 1965, when the remaining four decrees were promulgated. Moorman acknowledged that he and some others enjoyed the dignity and colour on such occasions, 'But not all of the observers felt like this. Some found them very distasteful, as if they emphasised all that they most disliked in Roman Catholicism . . . On this occasion I noticed that, although we were all supplied with exquisitely printed copies of the service, some of the observers took no part in it, not even joining in the Lord's Prayer.'[171] For Moorman, as for Irina Findlow, the most moving part of the ceremony was the lifting, by Paul VI and the Ecumenical Patriarch Athenagoras, of the anathemas and excommunications dating back to 1054. Irina remarked that she was near enough to notice that the Pope had tears in his eyes when he embraced Metropolitan Meliton of Heliopolis. Speaking to

---

169 Pope Paul VI, Address 4 December 1965, in J. Moorman, *Vatican Observed*, London: Darton, Longman and Todd, 1967: 207.
170 Moorman: 211–12.
171 Moorman: 179.

her husband, she said: 'you looked at me silently, we were too moved to speak'.[172]

The third ceremony was 8 December, the feast of the Immaculate Conception, when an open-air service was held on the steps of St Peter's. The Pope sent messages to various categories of peoples: rulers, men of thought and science, artists, women, workers, the sick and poor, and youth.

Thus ended the Second Vatican Council (1962–5).

---

172 Irina Findlow, *Journey Into Unity*, London: New City, 1975: 98.

4

A Visible Sign in Rome

Despite the uncomfortable relationship between Anglicans and Catholics in England, it was from that country mainly that the initiative was taken to establish in Rome a permanent presence of the Anglican Communion. Thus the Anglican Centre was founded the year after the ending of the Second Vatican Council, in 1966.[173] This chapter will reflect on the beginnings of the Anglican Centre in Rome and, in a more or less chronological way, trace its history over the period of its first four directors, up to 1995.

In some respects this chapter is about nuts and bolts, or more precisely about books and courses, electricity bills and rent, politics and planning and a host of other details which might tend to bore the reader. But there is another depth to be plumbed and it is the serious business of two great communions meeting for the first time, of popes and archbishops creating Common Declarations, and of interesting personalities interacting in the search for unity. Confessional differences are given a context and diversity is found to have a role in unity.

---

173 On the occasion of the blessing and opening of the new Anglican Centre in Rome, 12 February 1999, John Paul II reflected on Archbishop Michael Ramsey establishing the Centre in 1966 as 'a very visible sign in Rome of the commitment of the whole Anglican Communion to the dialogue that was to be undertaken with the Catholic Church'. *Information Service* 1999/1: 13.

Idea of an Anglican Centre

As early as September 1963 Bernard Pawley suggested to Lambeth the idea of an Anglican Centre in Rome. 'It is evident to me,' he wrote, 'that when the Council is over there will be scope and opportunity, if not an actual request, for an Anglican officer in Rome, and an Anglican Centre. Now is the time to be planning. The Romans would welcome it.'[174] A year later he raised the matter again,[175] and in his final report of 30 December 1964 he tells of his conversation with Cardinal Bea when he expressed his hope that one day there would be established in Rome an Anglican institute in some form. Soon after his arrival in January 1965, Findlow met with Willebrands who warmly welcomed Pawley's idea of a Centre, saying he would commend the use of it to seminarians and others in Rome interested in Anglican studies.[176]

Archbishop Ramsey wanted to include the entire Communion in planning and supporting the Centre. Bishop Ralph Dean, Executive Officer of the Anglican Communion, wrote to the Primates and Metropolitans of the Anglican Communion in December 1965. 'I am writing at the urgent request of His Grace, the Archbishop of Canterbury,' he said, 'to solicit your much needed interest and support in a plan to set up an Anglican Centre in Rome.'[177] At that time the idea was to purchase the building on Via Napoli, adjacent to St Paul's Within-the-Walls, at a cost of about £40,000.

By year's end John Moorman, widely regarded as the real founder of the Centre, John Satterthwaite, who was responsible for the legal work surrounding the setting up of the Centre in his capacity as secretary to the Council on Foreign Relations at Lambeth, and John Findlow expressed a preference for the apartment offered them in the Palazzo Pamphilj, comprising

---

174 Pawley report 79: 20 September 1963.
175 Pawley report 120: 11 May 1964.
176 Findlow report: 16 February 1965.
177 Letter of 15 December 1965. Lambeth Palace Library, Ramsey papers 70, 1965 'Anglican Centre in Rome'.

10 rooms and 2 bathrooms at a rent of L200,000 (£150) per month, including rates. Agreement was reached on 14 January 1966 when John Findlow met with Principessa Orietta Donna Pamphilj, her husband Don Frank Pogson Doria Pamphilj and their administrator.

The Doria Pamphilj Family

The Doria Pamphilj family were generous supporters of the Anglican Centre from its very beginning because they saw it as an important ecumenical venture, well before the word 'ecumenism' had become at all fashionable. Eventually Don Frank would become a board director of the Centre, and the Principessa a vice-president. This remarkable family received its princely title from Emperor Charles V of Spain in 1547, and demonstrated great strengths in the face of enormous challenges. For instance, Principessa Orietta's parents, Prince Filippo Andrea VI and his wife, Gesine – his Scottish nurse whom he met when convalescing in Switzerland – were both strongly anti-Fascist, so much so that Mussolini banished the Prince to a remote part of southern Italy, and changed the name of the little street which edged its way alongside the palace, from Vicolo Doria to Vicolo della Fede. Gesine stood staunchly at his side, refusing to turn over her wedding ring, as Italian women were required to do in order to finance Mussolini's Abyssinian campaign. Their teenage daughter, Orietta, hid with friends in Trastevere during their exile.

Once Italy was liberated, Prince Filippo was appointed mayor of Rome, and it was during this time that he managed to have the name 'Vicolo Doria' restored to the street adjacent to the palace. Orietta joined the Catholic Women's League that ran canteens for the advancing Allied forces, and it was during this time that she met Lieutenant-Commander Frank Pogson, a commander of a destroyer that sailed into Genoa. They fell in love. Before the prince died he gave his blessing to the marriage, with just one request, that the name Doria Pamphilj should not lapse. The marriage took place in London in 1958.

I spoke with Jonathan, their son, about the support his

parents gave to so many ecumenical causes, such as *Foyer Unitas,* the Ladies of Bethany,[178] the Anglican Centre and the *Centro pro Unione.*[179] He described his father, a wartime convert, as an intelligent, devoted yet critical Catholic. This openness he passed on to his wife. Jonathan, and his sister Gesine, therefore, were raised in an atmosphere of openness to the goodness of people and churches, never seeing Anglicans and Catholics in terms of their differences. 'Our commitment to these causes,' Jonathan said, 'matches that of our parents. On this my sister and I will never falter. We believe in bringing people together.'

Frank died in 1998, and Orietta in 2000, shortly after receiving the 'Order of the British Empire' (OBE) from Queen Elizabeth II, in recognition of her services to British charities.

Setting up the Centre

John Moorman wasted no time in seeking help for the Centre, approaching PECUSA and Churches in Canada and Australia. England was providing for the Anglican representative in Rome.

---

178 The Ladies of Bethany, a religious congregation founded in Holland in 1919, looked for an opportunity to do ecumenical work in Rome long before ecumenism had much of a place in Catholic circles. In conjunction with *Foyer Unitas* they did two things: alert Catholics to the problems of a divided Church, and act as helpers and tour guides to non-Catholic visitors to Rome. As a young lady, Orietta heard a talk given by one of the sisters on their work; thereafter she became an enthusiastic supporter of them. As from 1956 they had an apartment in the Collegio Pamphilj on Via del Plebiscito, but with the calling of the Second Vatican Council the Sisters were requested to care for the wives of the observers. They asked Frank and Orietta for rooms for 25 guests and quarters for themselves and their assistants. Space was found in the Collegio Innocenziano where *Foyer Unitas* and the Friars of the Atonement had their offices. The two surviving sisters ended their work in Rome in 1992, retiring to Holland.

179 The Friars of the Atonement, also based at the Collegio Innocenziano on Via Santa Maria dell'Anima 30 since 1962, edited the English edition of the *Foyer Unitas* ecumenical review from 1948 to 1968. It was in 1968 that they established there the *Centro pro Unione,* which has developed as an invaluable ecumenical resource.

An appeal was also made through the papers for £5000. Mrs Mildred Duggins, widow of the late Episcopal vicar of St Paul's, and Father Peter Searle were both generous, the Dorias paying for the setting up of the kitchen. Mildred later became the first librarian.

As well as establishing the Centre, there was the matter of its ongoing sponsorship and supervision. Thus, in April 1966 the Consultative Body of the Anglican Communion, meeting in Jerusalem, agreed to sponsor the Centre. Its executive officer, Bishop Ralph Dean, was the first chairman of the Centre's council. John Findlow, secretary to the Commission on Roman Catholic Relations at Lambeth and representative of the Archbishop of Canterbury in Rome, was the first director. He, Irina and their daughter Anna moved from the flat at the American Church to the Centre in April of 1966. Their other daughter, Maria, lived in the Findlows' flat in Lambeth Palace.

The library was John Moorman's chosen project. The first shipment of books arrived in late October 1966, the students from the North American College helping Mildred to catalogue them. Over a number of years John, back in England, shipped 6000 volumes to Rome, according to his diary of 2 October 1970. Henry Chadwick was later to check the library's needs and Canon John Halliburton monitored accessions. Lady Fisher gave 189 of the late Archbishop's books in 1973, and John Moorman's widow bequeathed near to £100,000 to the Centre.

Visit of Archbishop Ramsey to Rome

On 22 March 1966 Ramsey (Archbishop 1961–74) presided at the inauguration of the new Diocese of Gibraltar in a service at All Saints' in Rome, and dedicated the Anglican Centre, expressing himself in these words:

> The Anglican Communion cherishes the Holy Scriptures and the Catholic Creeds. In history, it values the lessons of the Reformation of the sixteenth century, and it values no less the continuity which it claims with the ancient Church. In

spirituality, it learns from saints and teachers of its own, while it also tries to learn from saints and teachers of every period in the West and in the East. In theology, it learns from the Scriptures, the ancient fathers and the liturgy, while it strives to use whatever light is shed by modern knowledge upon the understanding of man and the world. The Anglican student is often a debtor to writers within the Roman Catholic Church. This Centre is an attempt to repay that debt by making available the resources of Anglican learning to any who will come and enjoy them.[180]

The Centre had a twofold function. Catholic students wanting to know more about Anglicans, have use of it. Its second purpose was to offer courses for Anglicans, relying in part on the resources of Rome. From earliest times the Anglican Centre enjoyed good relations with the *Centro pro Unione* and the Venerable English College.

Archbishop Ramsey stayed as the Pope's guest at the English College. From there he went to the Sistine Chapel on the morning of 23 March to meet with Pope Paul VI. The following day they prayed together at St Paul's Outside-the-Walls, after having signed the *Common Declaration,* which we will return to in Chapter 6. It was as they said good-bye in front of St Paul's that the Pope took off his episcopal ring and placed it on the ring finger of the Archbishop's hand.[181] It was the ring given

---

180 'Address at Opening of New Anglican Centre, 22 March 1966.' Lambeth Palace Library, Ramsey Papers 1966, Vol 106: 142.

181 Where did Paul VI get the idea of presenting his ring to the Archbishop? On his deathbed in January 1926 Cardinal Mercier of Malines gave his pastoral ring to Lord Halifax. (R. Loonbeek-J. Mortiau, *Un Pionnier Dom Lambert Beauduin*, Louvain-la-Neuve 2001: 504. In a conversation with Jean Guitton on 8 September 1950, the then Monsignor Montini (later Paul VI) said: 'Je me souviens de ce geste symbolique si beau: le Cardinal mourant qui remet à Lord Halifax, le noble anglican, son anneau pastoral. C'est un symbole sublime' (Jean Guitton, *Dialogues avec Paul VI*, Paris 1967: 25). No doubt Paul VI recalled this conversation when he was saying his farewell to Archbishop Ramsey at St Paul's.

Montini by the people of Milan when he was their archbishop. Ramsey was deeply moved by the gesture; so was Paul VI by the whole event. After the Archbishop's death his wife, Joan, gave the ring to Archbishop Runcie, and it continues to be worn by his successors whenever they visit Rome.

Owen Chadwick recounts the story of an open forum the Archbishop enjoyed with the students of the Venerable English College. One asked: 'What do you consider the most annoying trait shown by English Catholics?' He replied: 'The natural inferiority complex of any minority group, spiced with a certain – one might say –bumptiousness.'[182]

Returning to the story of the Centre, the first meeting of its council was held, 3–5 October 1966, under the presidency of Bishop Dean, with 12 members in attendance. He made the point that the Archbishop of Canterbury's representative to the Holy See also represented the whole Anglican Communion. Business included finance and the drawing up of a constitution. On 5 October the council had a special audience with the Pope, the Bishop of Ripon speaking on their behalf. Paul VI expressed 'the hope of perfect communion between the two churches and indicating a formula for the future along the lines of mutual acquaintance preparing the way for love and love, in its turn, leading to union. Will it be thus? We hope so.'[183]

The official opening took place the same day, 5 October 1966. Cardinal Willebrands spoke on the importance and impact of the visit of the Archbishop of Canterbury, including one immediate result: the establishing of the Centre. He said:

> The Centre has been inaugurated, perhaps we may say twice – first by the presence and prayer of His Grace the Archbishop of Canterbury, and secondly today officially and practically put to work by the Anglican delegation which has come here. This Centre will contribute by research, by studies, by

---

182 Owen Chadwick, Owen: 322–3.
183 The exact words of the address can be found in *Information Service* 1967/1: 17.

conversation, to the dialogue which will be developed in the immediate future. It will contribute by personal contact, by thought, by prayer.[184]

First Director of Anglican Centre: Canon John Findlow (1966–70)

As already mentioned, John Findlow and his wife began residing in the Palazzo Doria Pamphilj in April 1966. He did not leave any comprehensive reports of his work in Rome, neither as an observer at the Vatican council nor as the first director of the Anglican Centre. Virginia Johnstone was his secretary both at Lambeth, and at the Centre for a short time, until Maria, John's daughter, took over the Rome secretarial position in November of his first year.

John was a brilliant linguist and, according to John Satterthwaite, an artistic man who was not at all ambitious. He would prefer having people to tea, rather than at a committee meeting. As it turned out the three jobs were too much for him, especially the dual responsibilities of London and Rome. The Centre, still in its embryonic stage, made great demands and since his first ecumenical love was Orthodoxy, adjusting to the ways of Rome was culturally and religiously all the more difficult.

His ire was aroused, and he let it be known, after Paul VI ordained 16 Beda College deacons to the priesthood, five of whom were converts from Anglicanism, in the Sistine Chapel on 25 January 1967. John wrote to Cardinal Bea remarking that it would have been better if the Pope had made no reference to better links with Anglicans at an ordination when he was re-ordaining several Anglican priests who were referred to as 'ministers' by certain Catholic spokesmen. He regarded the person, place and time as both undiplomatic and not in accord with the new ecumenical spirit. Such a conjunction, he said,

---

184 Translation of speech of the Right Revd Mgr J. G. M. Willebrands at the Inaugural Meeting of the Anglican Centre in Rome on 5 October 1966 (original in French). Anglican Centre archives.

inevitably raises doubts about the sincerity of Roman Catholic involvement in the serious dialogue which began so promisingly. After all, only last March the Archbishop and his entourage were received by Pope Paul in the Sistine Chapel and not as 'strangers and foreigners' (Ephesians 2.19). The Holy Father's action yesterday in the same place could and no doubt will be seen as a retrospective weakening of that welcome so significant for the furthering of future family relationships.[185]

The first signs of dissatisfaction with John as director surfaced at a stormy meeting in December 1968, when he was told, 'that it had been decided that there should now be a new director of the Centre, a theologian, preferably from the United States'.[186] The Americans, who provided most of the money, wanted a more businesslike operation, and so they 'pushed' him.

Within a few days of their arrival in London in April 1970, John took ill with encephalitis and was admitted to hospital, unconscious. The Archbishop of Canterbury and Cardinal Heenan both visited him. He died on 14 May and was buried at Chorleywood from the chapel at Lambeth Palace. During the trying weeks of his last illness the Church Commissioners requested the removal of the Findlow possessions from the Lambeth flat. Fortunately the Findlows had bought a house in Oxford, so Irina had a home to go to after John's untimely death.

Second Director: Canon Harry Reynolds Smythe (1970–81)

With the appointment of Canon Harry Smythe as the second director of the Anglican Centre, the status of the director changed from that of personal representative of the Archbishop of Canterbury to that of 'representative in Rome of the Anglican Communion'. He was from Melbourne, Australia, most

---

185 Anglican Centre archives.
186 Irina Findlow, *Journey Into Unity*, London, New City: 1975: 113.

recently pastor of St James parish and a teacher at Trinity College, and earlier a DPhil graduate of Oxford.

At his first audience with Paul VI he was told 'You may have access to me at any time for matters concerning the Anglican Centre and the Anglican Church.' He presented the Pope with two gifts. The first was a Book of Prayers of Queen Elizabeth I, published privately by Miss Barbara Simonds of Cornerstone Library who had requested that a copy be given to the Pope in the name of the Centre. The second was from the Dean of Durham who had heard from Pawley of Paul VI's interest in the Venerable Bede. The Pope had asked if a good life of Bede existed. The Chapter prepared an album with photos of the Galilee Chapel of the Cathedral which houses Bede's tomb and presented it to Paul VI, with a copy of Professor Hamilton Thompson's 1935 book of Essays, written on the occasion of the 12th centenary of Bede's death.

Canonization of the English martyrs

The canonization of the English martyrs in November 1970 stirred Smythe to rebuke the Vatican for ignoring the fact that many Anglican martyrs also 'gave telling proof of moral heroism'.[187] He saw an inappropriateness in the canonization happening exactly 400 years after Pius V issued the bull *Regnans in Excelsis,* excommunicating and deposing Queen Elizabeth I. Many historians, he said, saw the historic event as an awful blunder which continues to overshadow Anglican–Catholic relations. The Archbishop of Canterbury in his Christmas greetings to the Pope remarked on Paul VI's warm and friendly feelings expressed towards Anglicans on the occasion of the canonization. Anglicans, he said, reciprocate 'in the hope that one day there will be between us a consummated unity

---

187 See also Patrick Smith, *A Desk in Rome*, London: Collins, 1974: 26–7, where similar comment is made, adding that, unfortunately, the Anglican Church has no canonization process 'and therefore the Roman Catholics hold an advantage in heavenly accolades'.

which conserves all that has been true and good in our several traditions during the days of our separation'.[188] Auberon Waugh saw the canonization as a mistake of the leadership, and an unnecessary event of triumphalism.[189]

Smythe working his way into the Centre

Harry assessed the Centre as having an immense symbolic presence in Rome, without making any marked or immediate impact on the Catholic Church. What can one man do, he questioned, without adequate finances?[190] He decided to approach the Reverend Lord Beaumont of Whitley for assistance, who responded on 23 November 1970:

> I do believe that in the end all ecclesiastical ventures – and there are far too many of them – get what they need, and frequently more than they deserve, whereas there are endless causes outside the ecclesiastical scene which are starved of money . . . I am afraid that I must take the view so well put in Colin Morris's little book 'Include me out'.[191]

But in 1973 the Centre's financial situation was so serious that Smythe made an appeal to Bishop John Hines, presiding bishop in New York, who came up with half of the $6,000 requested.

Harry set out to make the Centre better known. He visited many institutions, including religious orders, colleges and universities, offering lectures in Rome, Assisi and Naples. He especially enjoyed regular contact with the Angelicum, having some involvement in its doctoral defences. He found a great deal of interest in Anglicanism around the city, including the Gregorian where he was involved in the organizing of an Anglican Studies programme. The first programme comprised 24 lectures on

188 Letter of Archbishop of Canterbury to Pope Paul VI: 15 December 1970. Anglican Centre archives.
189 Auberon Waugh in *The Spectator*, 14 November 1970: 597.
190 Director's Report: 10 November 1970.
191 Letter of reply in Anglican Centre archives.

'Anglican Theology Today', and the second 'Anglican Theology and Spirituality Today'. In 1976 the university advised him of a Vatican directive that non-Catholic professors could no longer teach at such institutions. Smythe even took it in private audience to Paul VI who was by now a very frail man. He raised it three times with John Paul II who, at his final audience in May 1981, said it would be resolved.

A particular interest of Smythe was 'The Associates Project for 12', a course designed for people who would 'gain and give'. In 1976 he sent a circular to the provinces inviting nominees, one applicant for the 1977 course of 21 days being George Carey, who later as Archbishop spoke very positively about this earlier experience.

Harry enjoyed his house in Assisi which allowed him weekend rest from duties in Rome. He was also very happy with his ecumenical relations in Assisi, particularly with Father Agostino, who was interested in Anglicans, though Harry was most displeased with John Satterthwaite who complained about not being consulted before he accepted membership of the governing body of the *Centro Ecumenico Nordico* in Assisi. Incensed, Harry wrote to John Howe of the Anglican Consultative Council, the good-humoured reply to the letter bringing a ready 'fix' to the problem – 'I have a feeling that it may have been written before one of your excellent gin and tonics, rather than after.' Care of the library was not a priority for him, which was upsetting for John Moorman. Harry immediately went on the defensive, to the point of wanting to write to the Archbishop of Canterbury questioning the suitability of the widely respected Bishop of Ripon as a member of the council. He was effectively restrained.

The frequent flow of letters to and from the Archbishop of Canterbury seem to have had a calming effect on Harry, though in one such letter in July 1973 the Archbishop chided him for mentioning to the Pope his possible visit to Rome and likely retirement. 'Don't say things like this unless I tell you to,' was the admonition. But Harry was not put off, suggesting to the Archbishop on hearing confirmation of his retirement plans, that he consider teaching at the Gregorian. The Archbishop declined.

Visit of Archbishop Donald Coggan to Rome

Formerly Bishop of Bradford, Donald Coggan accepted the position as Archbishop of York at the point when Ramsey was appointed to Canterbury. Archbishop Coggan was an evangelical, well educated and popular, who was regarded by the Queen and two Prime Ministers Harold Macmillan and Harold Wilson as a respected national figure. Hence his choice as Archbishop of Canterbury in 1974, a position he filled until 1980. There was a significant Catholic presence at his enthronement in January 1975, including Cardinal Willebrands, Leon Joseph Suenens and Gabriel Marty, Archbishop Cowderoy of Southwark and the Apostolic Delegate, Archbishop Bruno Heim.

He visited Rome 27–30 April 1977, and was the Pope's guest at the English College where, according to Smythe, the students enjoyed his open and frank manner, so unlike the Roman style of 'sitting on the fence'. He met for over an hour with Paul VI in his library on the morning of the 28th, going later in the day to dedicate the doors of St Paul's Inside-the-Walls. Cast in bronze, they symbolize the ecumenical encounter between Archbishop Geoffrey Fisher and Pope John XXIII on 2 December 1960, the first meeting of an Anglican archbishop and a Roman pontiff. They are the work of Dimitri Hadzi, an internationally known American sculptor, then a Roman resident and parishioner of St Paul's.

Evensong at St Paul's was jointly presided over by the Archbishop and Cardinal Willebrands. The Archbishop preached on a subject dear to his heart, the work of evangelism, alluding to the Pope's recent Apostolic Exhortation *Evangelii Nuntiandi*.[192] Joint evangelism might be weakened, he said, 'until we are able

192 English translation first published by the Vatican Polyglot Printing Press, and later by the Congregation for the Evangelization of Peoples, 8 December 1975.

to go to that work strengthened by our joint participation in the Sacrament of Christ's Body and Blood. The day must come when together we kneel and receive from one another's hands the tokens of God's redeeming love . . . The day must come, I said. In many places around the world, as those of us who travel know perfectly well, the day has already come . . . Has not the time, God's time, for such official sanction arrived? I think it has.'[193] The Cardinal and the SPCU were taken by surprise.

That evening 450 attended a reception in the Doria Pamphilj palace, including many important people. But the guest list included Signora Ida from the flower stall at the corner of Piazza Venezia, who was very overcome at the invitation, and said that it was not for people like her. But she did enjoy being presented to Archbishop Coggan, Harry recalls. After the reception, the Archbishop attended a dinner party in Harry Smythe's apartment, in the same palace.

On the 29th there was a service of prayer in the Sistine Chapel, the Pope and the Archbishop processing together to two thrones of equal dignity. Paul VI was very frail, this event being little more than a year before his death. After prayer they moved to the Pauline chapel for the reading in English by William Purdy of the *Common Declaration*. The Archbishop made a pen correction to the omitted citation marks before a biblical text. It was Smythe's opinion that the Archbishop's action was his subtle and kindly comment on the unwelcome intervention overnight from some Vatican official making a change to the draft and phoning the Archbishop to advise of it during the dinnerparty. Though the change was insubstantial – a phrase about 'what has been achieved' was removed – the principle did matter, altering a previously agreed Common Declaration. It is also worth remarking that the Declaration said 'The moment must soon come when the respective authorities must evaluate their (i.e. ARCIC's) conclusions.' But the wait was until 1991.

Harry Smythe spoke on Vatican Radio, honouring Paul VI's 80th birthday:

---

193 Anglican Centre archives.

Anglicans have special reasons to be thankful for Pope Paul. He is the first Pope in history, we believe, who has known a great deal about the Anglican family of Churches, and who has understood us.[194]

Owen Chadwick earlier wrote:

It is an understatement to say that Pope Paul VI knew more than any other Pope about the Church of England. He was the only Pope who had given the necessary time and trouble to understand the Church of England.[195]

A year after his visit to Paul VI, Archbishop Coggan was back in Rome to meet John Paul II. He felt the new Pope had three great attributes: warmth, strength and joy, though he seemed not to be ecumenical in the style of Paul VI.

Anglican Students in Rome

The story of Anglican students at the Venerable English College begins in October 1971 when Ronald Coppin, Secretary of the Committee for Theological Education in London, enjoyed a Sunday meal at the College in Rome. As he walked through the halls with the Rector, Monsignor Cormac Murphy-O'Connor, he caught sight of the pictorial history of the Venerabile, and in the chapel he learned of the *Te Deum* sung each time the community heard from England of another martyrdom.

The thought occurred to him that, in this age of improving relationships, if two Church of England ordinands spent a semester each at the college, it might help them gain and

---

194 Harry Smythe, 'Pope Paul VI's 80th birthday', Vatican Radio, 23 September 1977. Anglican Centre archives.
195 Owen Chadwick, 'The Church of England and the Church of Rome from the beginning of the nineteenth century to the present day' in *Anglican Initiatives in Christian Unity Lectures Delivered in Lambeth Palace Library 1966*, E. G. W. Bill, ed., London: SPCK, 1967: 104.

convey a better understanding of the two communions. Back in London, he contacted Bishop Alan Clark who, in turn, contacted the Rector, and it was agreed to begin a programme of two ordinands attending the college in the first semester. The Principals of St John's College, Nottingham and St Stephen's House, Oxford were willing to take part in the experiment, and so in September 1973 Nicholas Sagovsky from St John's College and Barry Hammett from St Stephen's House became students in the English College. Since then, with just a few exceptional years, English ordinands have spent the first semester at the Venerabile, as the chart indicates.

Anglican ordinands at the Venerable English College

1973–1974:	Barry Hammett and Nicholas Sagovsky
1975–1976:	Alan Coustic and Roger Stubbing (both Methodist)
1976–1977:	Michael Perrott and Peter Wadsworth
1977–1978:	Robert Atwell and Christopher O'Neill
1978 (for 3 months):	Arnold Browne and Christopher Beardsley
1978–1979:	Peter Atkinson and Michael Bartlett
1979–1980:	Perry Butler and Neil Thompson
1981–1982:	Keith Owen and Michael Tavinor
1982–1983:	Michael Fountaine and Peter Seal
1983–1984:	John Corbyn and John Davies
1984–1985:	Andrew Montgomerie and Martin Parrott
1985–1986:	Crispin Pemberton and Nicolas Von Malaisé
1987–1988:	Robert Beaken and Andrew Patterson
1988–1989:	Christopher Vipers and Andrew Willson
1989–1990:	Jonathan Boardman and Andrew Cain
1990–1991:	Simon Foster and David Nixon
1991–1992:	Ross Collins and Michael Everitt
1992–1993:	Adam Dickens and Anthony Hodgson

1993–1994:	Mark Bratton and Richard Jenkins
1994–1995:	David Allen and Andrew Allington
1995–1996:	Gordon Fyfe and Peter Packer
1997–1998:	Christopher Goble and Mark Williams
1998–1999:	Geoffrey Mumford and Mike Todd
1999–2000:	Kenneth Clark, Daniel Humphreys and Nicholas Leviseur
2000–2001:	Regan O'Callaghan, Justin White
2001–2002:	Mark Steadman and Simon Taylor
2002–2003:	Andrew Davison
2003–2004:	Neil Patterson
2004–2005:	Richard Carew and Timothy Harling
2005–2006:	Peter Anthony and John Seymour
2006–2007:	Jamie Hawkey and John Livesley

Each year Harry Smythe would hold a reception at the Centre for the staff and students of the English College in thanks for having the two Anglican students reside there. In 1977 he commented that henceforth there would be a regular exchange, the English College students going to Westcott House. Some-time earlier, two Episcopalian students from the General Theological Seminary in New York resided at the North American College, so overtures were made again in 1982, requesting the acceptance each year of two mature Episcopal students into the college. The Rector, Monsignor Charles Murphy, was unable to put anything in place; his successor, Monsignor Lawrence Purcell, made it clear he was not interested. Most recently, in 2002 Bishop Richard Garrard approached Monsignor Kevin McCoy, but again the matter was let rest.

Ordination of women

The question of the ordination of women was now more than just a topic of conversation. In the late sixties Coggan was a leading advocate, but as Archbishop he assumed a more cautious approach. Nevertheless, in February 1976 he wrote to the Pope as requested by the Church of England General Synod, explaining that while an important goal in Christian relations is visible unity, it will be manifested within a diversity of legitimate traditions.

> Sometimes what seems to one tradition to be a genuine expression of diversity in unity, will appear to another tradition to go beyond the bounds of legitimacy. Discussion within the Anglican Communion concerning the possibility of the ordination of women is at present just such an issue.[196]

Harry Smythe did not interpret 'diversity' so broadly, arguing that Anglicans could not consider the issue of the ordination of women in isolation from both the Christian tradition and the solemn commitment made between Pope Paul VI and the Archbishop of Canterbury in the *Common Declaration* of 1966. Going it alone is clearly excluded by this agreement, he maintained.

Exchanges between the Pope and the Archbishop continued, one letter being taken by hand to the Pope by Bishop John Howe, secretary-general of the Anglican Consultative Council. He came away from the meeting expressing surprise at the Pope's 'vehemence' on the subject. About three months after the 1978 Lambeth Conference the General Synod of the Church of England rejected a motion put forward by the Bishop of Birmingham, Hugh Montefiore, which sought the removal of the barriers to women's ordinations.[197]

Against this background a question presented itself: was Smythe becoming too Roman? Harry heard from the future presiding bishop of PECUSA: 'I don't see how anyone who

---

196 Letter of Archbishop Donald Coggan to Pope Paul VI: 10 February, 1976. Anglican Centre archives.
197 William Purdy, *The Search for Unity: Relations Between the Anglican and Roman Catholic Churches From the 1950's to the 1970's.* London, Geoffrey Chapman: 1996. See Chapter 25 'The ordination of women priests'.

holds your position as representative of the Anglican Communion could entertain your views on the ordination of women.' Harry's response was that the writer's view 'now shared by many, is really in my opinion, a concealed form of tyranny'. Bishop Thomas of Wangaratta (Australia) wrote on 4 October 1978, disagreeing with Harry, in language that only a fellow Australian would understand.

As his contract neared its end Smythe wrote a ten-page reflection on his term as director. As 'representative' of the Communion, Harry mused, he had to learn the job, with little or no ecclesiastical support except from the Archbishop of Canterbury and the responsible bishop. As 'ambassador' he interpreted his role as bearing witness to classical Anglicanism, and not as one whirled about by what is new. The Centre he saw as a 'great idea for which no one was really prepared to pay'. In Italy there was a great ignorance of the Anglican faith, with an interest in finding out more, though Rome, he felt, was especially ignorant of the Reformation, and so were 'victims of their own propaganda'.[198]

In farewell he received a message of thanks signed by all the Primates of the Anglican Communion, and a signed photo of Archbishop Coggan. Harry expected the offer of a position in England, since he had no desire to return to Australia, but Bishop Howe said he should be looking around himself. He felt abandoned. Harry departed Rome on Ascension Day 1981, after a Mass in the crypt of St Peter's offered by Monsignor Martin Molyneux, with 20 friends present. 'I set off to walk as a pilgrim to Canterbury; the journey was completed by stages always on foot, over a period of 10 years.' Harry assumed the position of Custodian of the library at Pusey House, Oxford, a position he filled from 1983 through to his retirement in 1994. He died on 22 July 2005.

---

198 Harry Smythe, 'Reflections and Queries After 11 years in Rome', 22 March 1981. Anglican Centre archives.

Third Director: Canon Howard Root (1981–91)

The third director of the Anglican Centre had already enjoyed a long involvement in Anglican–Catholic affairs. Canon Howard Root, Professor of Theology at the University of Southampton, first engaged in dialogue in 1961, becoming also an observer at Vatican II. He was a member of the Joint Preparatory Committee of ARCIC from 1967 and a member of ARCIC itself from 1970. He assumed his duties as director of the Centre on 1 October 1981, holding the position for ten years, remaining a member of ARCIC throughout. His wife, Celia, was paid £3,000 p.a. in recognition of the considerable assistance she gave to the Centre.

According to his first report in 1982 Root came face to face with one of the vagaries of Roman life. The Centre's electricity meters, having been papered over in the distant past, meant they had not been read for at least seven, if not ten, years. All this time ENEL had been paid on an 'estimate' basis, and since the bills were in the name of J. Findlow, the Centre was actually breaking the law. At this point, Root remarked, attending to bricks and mortar took up 75% of his time.

In the 1983 Week of Prayer for Christian Unity, the beatification of Sister Maria Gabriella Sagheddu at St Paul's Outside-the-Walls made a big impact on Howard. The postulator of the cause was anxious for Anglican participation in the ceremony, so six Anglican priests occupied the front row of St Paul's on the Pope's left. Even more memorable for Howard and Celia was the minibus journey on 22 April to Blessed Gabriella's community at Vitorchiano, near Viterbo, to participate in the first solemn liturgical celebration after her beatification. 'The ceremony was memorable by its simplicity and manifest spirit of prayer for unity. We are now concretely in touch with this community.' In his reporting Howard makes an interesting aside: 'I have given more time to this than I expected. The more I think about it the more important I believe it to be.'[199] What he learned from

---

199 Director's Report 1983. Anglican Centre archives.

this Catholic patroness of ecumenism was the importance of spiritual ecumenism. It is reported that Gabriella had never met an Orthodox, Anglican or Protestant, but she was convinced enough, from reading John 17, to offer her life for the unity of the Church.[200]

During the week of prayer for Christian unity the calls on the director are demanding. As a later director remarked, 'Rome tries to salve its ecumenical conscience, especially in unity week, by inviting us to give talks. The trouble is there's such a big flurry.' One event Howard particularly enjoyed was preaching at a Choral Evensong at the English College, arranged by the two Anglican ordinands resident there. He also preached at the North American College where, he judged, 'a new relationship is being forged'. Later he gave a lecture on Anglican spirituality at the Beda College, the first time, he said, an Anglican had been invited to do anything of this kind, which is not entirely correct. Harry Smythe, for one, had spoken there in November 1971 on the ARCIC *Agreed Statement on Eucharistic Doctrine*. There are occasions when some mischievous Vatican official introduces a sour note, as happened at the papal Mass at the conclusion of unity week in 1985. The abbot of St Paul's had asked Howard to read one of the prayers of intercession, but a day or two before, the invitation was withdrawn. The year following, Root reports, the invitation was extended again, and not withdrawn. He assessed things philosophically: 'development continues, and every year brings something new'.

Seminars assumed an important place during Root's time, though more than once he lamented the fact that running the Centre and conducting seminars was just too taxing on a director. He secured the services of a young man from England for ten weeks through the generosity of SPCK, who undertook the first inventory of the library. He worked closely with Celia Root, who was a very efficient administrator. It was becoming clear that the Centre needed a full-time assistant, especially if

---

200 See the encyclical *Ut Unum Sint* of John Paul II, Vatican City: Libreria Editrice Vaticana, 1995: n 27 and footnote 50.

the mooted 'Friends of the Centre' was to develop, requiring a variety of communications and so on. In fact, the introductory letter to the Friends would be sent in October of 1983. Eventually an appointment was made of an assistant for five months, sponsored by SPCK and USPG, and he catalogued the ARCIC papers given by Bishop John Moorman.

It was policy to pay expenses of seminar participants, and for those coming from the third world to pay their fares, too. Fortunately in 1982 Bishop Arthur Walmsley of Connecticut gave $14,000, and the year following $15,000, enough to cover these costs for three years. Then the primates of those attending were approached to give assistance for the years 1986–8; and there was the hope that the newly launched Friends might help, too. Between 1982 and 1986, 56 bishops and priests, not-self-selected but nominated by the primates, participated in the seminars.

Within a year or two, 'issues' started to emerge, such as the wish of women priests to attend. Canon Dorothy Daly, a Canadian, applied for the 1987 seminar, Rev Brian Prideaux, an official in the Canadian scene, negotiating on her behalf. The response from Root, supported by the executive committee, was in the negative because of 'our special relationship with the Holy See . . . our seminars depend on taking Rome as it is and not perhaps as we might like it to be'. In reply, Brian Prideaux remarked: 'A case could be made for Rome taking us as we are. If they cannot I wonder how far we can expect to get in our dialogue with them.'[201] The day arrived soon enough when the composition of seminars would change to include clergy and laity, women and men.

Writing for the Friends Newsletter of Autumn 1984 Root suggested that Anglicans might like to learn from the Congregation for the Doctrine of the Faith (CDF). The work of theologians, for instance, could be looked at by a competent body, which might say after serious study and discussion: 'We are terribly sorry, but it seems to us that Professor X, or Canon Z, seems

---

201 Director's Report March 1986. Anglican Centre archives.

rather to have departed from the Anglican understanding and expression of the Christian faith.'

Visitors to the Centre were welcomed. One particularly memorable visit in 1984 was that of Bishop Keith Sutton and his Catholic geographical counterpart, Bishop Howard Tripp, auxiliary of Southwark. Working closely together in south London they decided on a joint visit to Rome. Howard Root remarked: 'an Anglican and a Roman Catholic bishop come together to our Centre at their own request, and come to speak and to hear. When they left us we were full of hope.'[202] One who became a particularly good friend of the Roots and of the Centre was the President of the Republic, President Francesco Cossiga, a man well read in classical Anglican literature.

In his latter years Root did not produce written reports, but gave oral summaries to the directors at their meetings. ARCIC occupied him quite a deal. The year 1986 was the 20th anniversary of the Centre and to mark the occasion a function was held which Cardinal Willebrands attended with most of the SPCU staff. The Pope received the council of the Centre in private audience, as did President Cossiga. Owen Chadwick gave a lecture to an audience of over 100 on 'Archbishop Michael Ramsey, the Pope and the Patriarch of Moscow'.[203]

Friends of the Anglican Centre

There was an informal meeting at the British Embassy to the Holy See in Rome in May 1983, exploring the possibility of establishing a Friends group. The broad purpose of the Friends, if organized, would be to make the Centre better known and to assist it by raising funds. A meeting took place in London on 6 November 1984, Sir Mark Heath[204] taking the chair, with three life members being inscribed immediately. On 2 April 1985 the Friends were officially launched at Lambeth, their principal

---

202 Director's Report 1983–1984. Anglican Centre archives.
203 Director's Report 1983–1986. Anglican Centre archives.
204 Sir Mark Heath died on 28 September 2005.

activity defined as the advancement of Christian unity by the support of the Anglican Centre. After the official launching the first meeting of the English Committee took place in Church House on 11 October 1985.

By 1990 between £30,000 and £40,000 had been subscribed by approximately 450 members and, among other things, the money financed employment of an assistant for the Centre for several months during each of the five years. Members gave generously, enabling the Friends in 1991 to make a donation of £25,000 to the endowment fund. They purchased office equipment, repainted rooms, mended and painted windows and helped pay for the replacement of the electrical wiring. In 2005 there were 170 Friends in Britain.

Eventually the Friends had the Centre's library named the 'Moorman Library', the bishop's pastoral staff being given on permanent loan. In October 1997 it was reclaimed for display in Ripon Cathedral.

Branches of the Friends do exist around the world, in Australia, Canada and Japan. In the USA the official name is The American Friends of the Anglican Centre in Rome.

The problem of finance and the restructuring of the Centre

Finance, like staffing, was a never-ending problem for the Centre. To make matters worse, in the late eighties an increasing number of regular donors began cutting their regular contributions, including the traditional major giver, ECUSA. Reports were commissioned on what to do about the Centre and how to finance it. There was the Chadwick Report of 1987, which died a natural death, followed by Canon Christopher Hill's paper of April 1989 which suggested a separation of the academic and representative functions of the Centre, relocating the library elsewhere, perhaps at the Angelicum.

Also in 1989, the Primates' Committee set up a special working party under the chairmanship of Bishop Ted Luscombe, primate of Scotland, which made a strongly stated case for the Centre's importance and continuation. The working party made three principal recommendations: to replace the present very large council by a small governing body, over a local management committee; to establish an endowment to secure the future of the Centre; to offer more courses alongside the present seminar for senior church leaders.

An analysis of the Centre's financial situation makes scary reading. In 1984 the grant was £39,000, the peak year being 1987 with £57,000, and the projected allowance for 1991 was £40,000 while its current running costs were in the vicinity of £58,000. It was a moment of crisis. Bishop Eric Kemp drafted a statement that was approved by the Executive Committee on 20 April 1990. It said that if stable funding could not be found then the Centre should close in September 1991.[205]

Canon Stephen Platten, who now begins to emerge as a significant figure in the Centre's ongoing life, 'said that in Rome the symbolic nature of closing the Anglican Centre would be greater than is generally realized. The signals sent out by such an action could be very serious for Anglican–Roman Catholic relations.'[206] He made the point that in the Roman way of doing things ecumenism is done at and from the Centre, and that is where the Anglican Communion ought to have a presence.

Platten, as the Archbishop of Canterbury's secretary for Ecumenical Affairs, accompanied Archbishop Runcie to the Primates' meeting in Cardiff where the Luscombe Report was largely endorsed. The Archbishop of Canterbury, in October 1990, wrote to the members of the Council of the Anglican Centre, giving his support to its continuance and outlining the structural proposals. A meeting was held on 25 November 1990 to put the proposals into action.

The *first* matter of concern was the replacing of the existing council of about 24 members by a governing body, which today numbers six. The first chairman was the Right Revd Mark

---

205 Unsigned paper on behalf of The Executive Committee, 1 May 1990. Anglican Centre archives.
206 Anglican Centre Executive Committee minutes: 19–20 April 1990. Anglican Centre archives.

Santer, also co-chairman of ARCIC. Today the chairman is the Right Revd Stephen Platten, Bishop of Wakefield. The Revd Barry Nichols, competent in financial matters, is also very important to the Centre's continuance.[207]

The *second* issue was finances, given that the annual grant of £40,000 was to be phased out over the next three years. Funding would be the Centre's own responsibility as from 1994. So, at the end of 1991 an appeal was launched, with John Haddon as its director, to raise in excess of £1.5 million as a permanent endowment which, if achieved, would generate an annual income of £60,000 p.a. The advertising included a message from the Archbishop of Canterbury and the Bishop of Birmingham, the patrons listed, including the President of Italy and the present and past Archbishops of Canterbury. John Haddon died in 1993; his place was taken by Major Ingleby Jefferson until mid-1995. In fact, only about £300,000 was raised, principally in the UK and USA; this sum included £100,000, the bequest of Mrs Moorman. Any subsequent enhancing of the endowment fund is likely to be through bequests, such as that given by Bishop Moorman's widow.

Meeting the annual running costs is the preoccupation of the governors. In the early nineties they amounted to about £50,000 p.a., but now they are in the region of £150,000 p.a. Barry Nichols is the chairman of the appeal committee.

A *third item* was to arrive at a policy regarding courses that would be doubly profitable, to the participants and to the Centre. St George's College, Jerusalem, was taken as a model. Advantaged by its presence in the Holy Land, it offered Bible study in its setting, courses on history and archaeology, Islam and Judaism, and their relations with Christianity. Fees covered the cost of the courses but also provided income to make the college self-sustaining. The idea was for the Rome Centre to take advantage of its Roman location, offering courses that would be comprehensive enough to attract students from around the

---

207 Barry was awarded the Cross of St Augustine in October 2005 for his services to the Anglican Centre.

world. ROMESS was established as a subsidiary of CORAT of Canterbury, offering a two-week course once a year on the Rome campus of Loyola University, Chicago.[208] The course asks what the concept of 'God' means for different persons worldwide and what it means for Christians. Visits to historic sites and museums form a major part of the course. The sum of £50,000 is the annual income, making a profit for the Centre of about £5000. The equivalent programme in Canterbury is called CANTESS. Though the courses continue, the association with Loyola does not.

When Bishop Mark Santer stood down as chairman, Bishop Frank Griswold II, presiding bishop of the United States, assumed the presidency. He found his workload too great, so while remaining a governor, he handed the chairmanship in May 2001 to Stephen Platten, later the Bishop of Wakefield, who continues in this post. It was deemed appropriate to have a representative of the Far East, the Archbishop of Hong Kong nominating Ms Fung-yi Wong, who is registrar of the Province of Hong Kong and a lawyer. In November 1991 the governing body met to establish itself as a company and also to set in place a local management committee. It meets twice yearly, November in Rome, and May in London or New York. Since December 1992 the Centre is properly constituted as a charity in Britain and in Italy.

A *fourth* issue connected with the restructuring of the Centre's government and funding, was the matter of the suitability of the present location and staffing. Both of these points would be addressed during the time of the next two directors.

---

208 The Rome campus of Loyola was established in 1962 to provide undergraduate studies. It is located in Via Massimi.

Archbishop Robert Runcie and Pope John Paul II

Robert Runcie's Anglican religious inclination became evident in his youth. Baptized in St Luke's, Crosby, a church of the evangelical tradition, he found attendance at services there dull and uninspiring. His confirmation and first communion at age 14 took place in Anglo-Catholic St Faith's where worship was much more attractive to him, so St Faith's became his regular parish church.

On his move to Canterbury (Archbishop 1980–91) from St Albans in 1979, where he had been bishop for nine years, Runcie was viewed as a contrast to the evangelicalism of Archbishops Coggan and Stuart Blanch, the latter the Archbishop of York. Margaret Duggan speaks of him as 'a moderate Catholic inclined towards radical views, though occasionally more conservative – as in the matter of the ordination of women'.[209]

His first meeting with John Paul II was in the papal nuncio's house in Accra, Ghana on 16 May 1980. It was here that he suggested to the Pope that he might visit Canterbury, an event that happened in 1982. Preparations for the visit appear to have been a tedious process. It was intended to extend an official joint invitation from Anglicans and Catholics, but Hume jumped the gun when, at Castel Gandolfo and on the spur of the moment, he asked the Pope to visit England. Runcie was on a Greek cruise at the time, so Anglican follow-up was in the hands of Christopher Hill who became a little tetchy over a procedure gone wrong. Discussion then focused on what kind of service would be appropriate in Canterbury Cathedral, which came down to either a Eucharist or a Liturgy of the Word. Henry Chadwick spent four days in Rome dealing directly with the Pope and the curia on the preferred service, which ended up being a Liturgy of the Word. It seems that some fairly elementary questions were raised which Chadwick was more than capable of handling, including the role of the Queen, the relations of church and

---

209 Margaret Duggan, *Runcie: The Making of an Archbishop*, London: Hodder and Stoughton, 1983: 40.

state, the Establishment of the Church of England, the Angli-can attitude to saints, and the ordination of women. Chadwick sums up: 'I came away from my interviews at the Curia with the impression that Anglicans have come to seem a bore to the top administrators of the Roman Catholic Church.'[210]

Assessments of the value of the visit vary. Purdy's assess-ment is that it had great value in drawing attention to the com-mon origins of Catholics and Anglicans. No Bishop of Rome had ever been in Britain, yet Gregory the Great sent a monk to found the church of Canterbury. Pawley was particularly impressed by the renewal of baptismal vows, which involved every Christian present. David Edwards spoke of the visit as 'potential and promise unfulfilled' and Andrew Brown as an event which 'marked a profound change in English self-under-standing: English patriotism had long been entwined with anti-Catholicism'.[211]

The Archbishop visited Rome in September 1989. Part of his address read:

> for over twenty years Anglicans and Roman Catholics have been re-discovering the unity they have always shared. We are beginning to receive from each other the gifts and treasures of our two traditions. We are learning the cost of growing into that more perfect unity which accords with our Lord's will.

Then, referring to the episcopal ring he was wearing, the gift of Paul VI to Archbishop Michael Ramsey in 1966, he continued: 'I wear it today as we rededicate ourselves to the search for visible and sacramental unity.' He presented the Pope with a painting by a distinguished contemporary English artist, Sonia Lawson, explaining that

> It is an interpretation of St Augustine's landing to evangelise

---

210 Humphrey Carpenter, *Robert Runcie: The Reluctant Archbishop*, London: Hodder and Stoughton, 1996: 241.
211 Christopher Hill in *Runcie on Reflection: An Archbishop Remembered*, Stephen Platten, ed., Norwich: Canterbury Press, 2000: 95.

the English at the command of your predecessor St Gregory the Great. In the painting Augustine and his monks, with dark hair representing the warm south, move forward with enthusiasm to our green northern island with its fair-coloured peoples. The bridge between them is the book of the Gospels. Its radiance illuminates. Its good news is gift.[212]

A copy of this painting hangs in the Centre, while the original hangs in the meeting room of PCPCU.

Runcie acknowledged that the action of some Anglican provinces in opening the priesthood and episcopacy to women seems to the Catholic Church to have gone beyond the bounds of legitimate diversity. He also recognized the need for a focus for the Christian community; it is found in the primacy of the Bishop of Rome, an insight that he attributed to ARCIC. On another occasion, reflecting on John Paul II, the Archbishop said: 'his ecumenism is strong on rhetoric, but not very good on substantial steps'.[213]

The year 1991 was the Silver Jubilee of the opening of the Centre by Archbishop Ramsey, and the completion of the term of office of Howard Root as director.

Fourth Director: Father Douglas Brown SSM (1991–5)

In the talk about 'recreating' the Centre, one suggestion was to invite a religious community to take over its administration. Thus, Douglas Brown, an Australian and a member of the Society of the Sacred Mission, founded in 1893 by Father Herbert Kelly, was appointed the fourth Director in September 1991. He was joined a few weeks later by Brother Andrew Murumatsu who would take care of the kitchen. The idea was that normally two members of the SSM would be in residence,

212 'The Meeting of Archbishop Runcie with Pope John Paul II' 30 September 1989. *Information Service* 71: 1989/III-IV: 114–15.
213 Humphrey Carpenter, *Robert Runcie: The Reluctant Archbishop*, London: Hodder and Stoughton, 1996: 234.

thus creating a priory; there might be a third member. Douglas rearranged the Centre to provide three bedrooms for members of the priory and three for paying guests. Having overnight guests belongs only to the Brown period, though it has been revived in the time of Bishop John Flack. In April 1993 Douglas reported for the previous year 83 overnight stays, giving an occupancy rate of 60%, a better average than any hotel, he suggested. In 1993 Ralph Martin, a Canadian, joined the priory, and stayed just over a year, as registrar of courses. He moved to All Saints' as locum, following the death of Peter Marchant, continuing to do just a little at the Centre so that the effort in solving its staffing problems was short-lived.

Things didn't always go smoothly. Early June 1992 Father Brown received a letter from Bishop Mark Santer[214] commenting on rumbles that had reached him from Anglican and Catholic sources about the lecture he gave a few months earlier, when Francis Sullivan SJ also spoke. Santer raised four areas of concern:

(1) Your acceptance, or otherwise, of the fundamental method of ARCIC in handling inherited areas of theological dispute.

(2) The injustice and unkindness evident in one who represents the Anglican Communion and the Archbishop of Canterbury, in calling the members of ARCIC I 'devious'.

(3) Your unawareness of the culture gap between the Anglo-Saxon style of doing business and the Roman style: in the case of the latter, blunt dissent means one is written-off, whereas dissent not so directly confrontative leaves an opponent's dignity intact.

(4) Your very negative assessment of the place of Councils in the Church's history, including a very simplistic reading of the case of Nestorius.

---

214 Bishop Santer's letter is dated 8 June 1992, and Father Brown's reply 15 June 1992. Anglican Centre archives.

Santer suggested that when he and Stephen Platten were next in Rome, 'the three of us might consult about your role in relation to various institutions and authorities'.

Douglas took the admonitions to heart, though he also rose in self-defence. He had little respect for 'diplomatic language', especially with respect to infallibility. And ARCIC, he claimed, is fair game since it offers a statement on the Church for discussion. 'If I am an official spokesman for the Anglican position(s) I can best do this by demonstrating a certain freedom of expression . . . I don't think that diplomatic niceties are so important.' Fundamentally, Douglas had a problem that related directly to his position in Rome.

As one director said of him: 'He was very cynical, even negative, about the Catholic Church.' This negativity was evident in his writings, including the newsletter, *ACR Centro*, where he spoke of 'the missives hurled from the hand of the Pope'. Elsewhere he remarked: 'There can be no doubt that for the Pope the Roman Catholic Church is the one, true, pure, apostolic Church, which has miraculously preserved the faith from the beginning.' Regarding the primacy he wrote: 'This is a foundational myth which is obviously designed to legitimise the use of power.'[215] In commenting on *Evangelium Vitae* he said: 'Light battles against darkness, good against evil, life against death, and the Pope against abortion.'[216] For an ambassador he could at times create blocks that were inappropriately undiplomatic.

Though Brown put effort into planning the courses, such as the Rome summer course and the Anglican leaders' conference, in his 1992 report he mentions that 27 attended the summer course, but very few attended the leaders' conference and there were just five at the ecumenical seminars. In 1993 the best response was given to the Rome course with 14 attending, and a maximum of five on any other seminar or course. With only three applying for the leaders' course, it was cancelled. He reported that the *ACR Centro* publication was well

---

215 *ACR Centro*. Vol. 3, No 3. July 1995: 3.
216 *ACR Centro*. Vol. 3, No 2. April 1995: 1.

received, though Sir Derek Pattinson and Virginia Johnstone of the English Friends considered that it needed writing in a less heavy, more popular style. They were right.

The Centre's location and finances

Talk of relocating the Centre had been going on for a long time, as if a move would be the 'solution' to its ongoing major problem, a lack of funds. The conversations already happening in 1970, but on a broader front, suggested a combining of the two Anglican churches and the Centre. John M. Krumm, bishop of the Convocation of American Churches in Europe, wanted to make 'a more coherent and effective impact on the city of Rome and the central seat of the Roman Catholic Church'. He saw value in unifying the two congregations, integrating the resources and personnel, creating a centre for research and study – and all of them together, physically, in one set of buildings. At a 1981 meeting of the council an extract from a 1977 statement was recalled: 'in the event of a union of the two Anglican congregations in Rome, the site of the Centre could be reconsidered'.[217]

With Father Martin SSM taking over the chaplaincy of All Saints' there was an agreement in principle in 1993 to move the Centre to the crypt of All Saints'. But by year's end the plan changed, in favour of an Anglican partnership in Rome. The chaplains of All Saints' and St Paul's would become assistant directors of the Centre. The director of the Centre would be associate rector of St Paul's and assistant priest at All Saints'. But then, the January 1995 *ACR Centro* reported that the Board of Directors at their November meeting decided that the Centre should remain at the Palazzo Doria Pamphilj, recommending closer co-operation among the three Anglican entities in the city.

As Brown's endtime drew near, and the decision had been

---

217 Minutes of the Council of the Anglican Centre: 22–24 March 1981.

made to stay in the palace, the governors were feeling more comfortable about planning the Centre's future. One choice they made was to redefine its role under the patronage of the Archbishop of Canterbury, with the director having an improved status: maybe he should be a scholar, a bishop and perhaps a member of ARCIC. The second was for Stephen Platten and Bill Franklin to jointly produce a statement of mission goals for the new director. Important in the selection and appointment was making sure that the director was seen as representing the whole Communion. To this end, Bishop Santer would write to all the primates.

Douglas Brown deserves a plaudit. He lived through a period of great insecurity at the Rome Centre, at a time when its future and its financial problems dominated more so than ever before. But for him, it might well have closed.

5

Not Simply Moving House

Despite the eventual decision to stay in the Palazio Pamphilj, the contract had expired and the premises re-zoned as office space, thus commanding a much higher rent. Gesene Doria Pamphilj did the Centre a great turn, offering a better and larger apartment in the palace, on the Piazza Collegio Romano side. The annual rent was beneficially calculated at £11,000 p.a. for nine years, renewable for a further nine. There were obvious advantages in moving to this new apartment, though the cost of renovating was then estimated between £50,000 and £100,000. The refurbishing and the relocating would occur in the time of the new director, Bruce Ruddock.[218]

Fifth Director: Canon Bruce Ruddock (1995–9)

After a bad experience on his visit to the Centre in 1994 which led Bruce to inscribe in his diary 'I never want to see the Anglican Centre again',[219] fate or providence intervened by way of an approach from Stephen Platten: 'Are you prepared to be short-listed for the director's job in Rome?' As it turned out, from October 1995, Bruce became the fifth director of the Centre and Vivien, his wife, the administrator.

Having been vicar of the parish of St Michael and All Angels

---

218 As the work on the new Centre was nearing completion, Bruce Ruddock reported that 'a new Anglican Centre in Rome will make a powerful statement about Anglican commitment to the search for Christian unity – we are not simply moving house'. 1998 Report.
219 Diary entry: 17 June 1994.

in Barnes, which was ordered and efficiently run, it was inevitable that this new position would be challenging. Little was prepared for the 1996 courses, they discovered, and cash flow problems remained, the place itself was inhospitable and there was the inevitable and challenging task of coming to terms with Rome.

Bruce and Vivien set out to convey an image of change, introducing new letterhead and visiting cards, refreshed publicity and a new leaflet on the Centre, and a new image in the magazine. Bruce relished the public relations aspect of his work, and succeeded in it. He enjoyed his contacts with the aged Cardinal Willebrands and Bishop Pierre Duprey, and he appreciated Cardinal Cassidy, President of PCPCU, whom he found a great support. 'Sometimes,' Bruce told me when we met on 7 February 2003, 'we felt that Roman Catholics loved us more than did the Anglican Communion. But, in England, he continued, Catholicism is so different. We have this sad history of sending one another to the stake.'

Bruce was intent on displacing old caricatures. For example, that the Catholic Church is a pyramid, with one man at the top who calls himself infallible, and that Anglicans are people who believe, decide and say what they like, and are generally not challenged by any kind of order or canonical obedience. A better beginning point, Bruce suggests, is that 'today there are two types of Christians: those who want unity and those who don't. You will find them in both our Churches . . . There are some places in Rome where you feel less welcome; but, in general, Rome is an extremely ecumenical place, and the atmosphere is very positive.'[220] Interestingly, Bruce prefers to be an ecumenical representative at the Eucharist than at any other form of service. 'It means we feel the pain. We don't hide it and pretend we're all one. We feel it and pray through it.'[221]

---

220 Pat Ashworth interviews Canon Bruce Ruddock. *Church Times* 12 February 1999: 13.
221 Ibid.

Archbishop Carey's First Visits to Rome

As with Archbishop Runcie's first encounter with the Holy Father, it was deemed appropriate for the first meeting between George Carey and Pope John Paul II to be something less than a full-blown visit; Archbishop Runcie had coincided with Pope John Paul II in Accra. In the case of Archbishop Carey the first encounter was more formal but still not a full visit. It was decided that the Archbishop should pay a formal visit to the Roman Catholic Church in Italy and that the papal meeting should take place alongside this. Accordingly a programme was set up in the summer of 1992, which included visits to Palermo, Venice and Milan. At Palermo, Cardinal Papallardo arranged visits to social projects and he also welcomed the Archbishop formally at a magnificent celebration of Solemn Vespers. This visit was made that much more dramatic by the Mafia assassination of Judge Falcone on the road between Palermo and the airport just a few days before! At Venice, Cardinal Ce welcomed the Archbishop, arranging cultural visits and again receiving him in St Mark's basilica for ecumenical prayers. In Milan, Cardinal Martini engaged with the Archbishop in theological discussion, notably at the main diocesan seminary, and there was a service too in the cathedral.

The meeting with the Holy Father did not take place in a propitious context. The Vatican response to *ARCIC I: The Final Report* in the previous autumn had been lukewarm. Furthermore, the Archbishop had, in the week before leaving for Rome, uttered some critical words in an interview with the *Sunday Telegraph* in London on Roman Catholic teaching on birth control. Despite this there was a positive meeting and a real engagement between the Pope and the Archbishop. They met for just under an hour and a cautious but hopeful *Common Declaration* was issued. This initial encounter prepared the way for the 1996 formal visit and for what became a record number of meetings between a Pope and an Archbishop of Canterbury. The Anglican Centre and the two Anglican churches in Rome played a key part in the visit as did Her Majesty's Ambassador to the Holy See, Mr Andrew Palmer, with whom the Archbishop stayed for his time in Rome. The Anglican Centre was well known to the new Archbishop since he had stayed there some years before when Principal of Trinity College in Bristol; he was already an enthusiast for Rome and a good friend of Professor Gerard O'Collins and other prominent Roman Catholic theologians.

From 3 to 6 December 1996 George Carey (1991–2002), the fifth Anglican Archbishop of Canterbury to visit the Pope, was hosted at the English College for his first full 'official' visit. In his address to John Paul II the Archbishop spoke of the 'absolute commitment both of myself personally and also of the Anglican Communion to the full, visible unity of God's Church'.[222] He went on to speak of the marks of separation and division and of the need to confront them. The Pope in reply spoke of the visits of Archbishops to Rome since the Vatican Council, and his own visit to Great Britain in 1982. 'Through these visits, and especially through the prayer which accompanies them, we have been reminded again and again that, even in our sad separation, Anglicans and Catholics have not ceased to be brothers and sisters in the one Lord.'[223] In the evening of the first day of the Archbishop's visit they celebrated Vespers at the Church of St Gregory on the Caelian Hill.

In their meeting on 5 December the Archbishop spoke very affirmatively of the work of ARCIC I and II which set the foundations for the desired full visible unity. The two Commissions, he said, have identified 'our fundamental agreement concerning the Holy Eucharist and Ministry, the doctrine of justification by faith; to say nothing of substantial progress in the way we see authority exercised in the Church and the forming of moral theology'.[224] Given this level of theological and ecclesiological convergence, a mutual recommitment to

---

222 Address of the Archbishop of Canterbury to John Paul II: 3 December 1996. *Information Service* 1997/I: 14.
223 Address of Pope John Paul II to the Archbishop of Canterbury: 3 December 1996: 15.
224 Address of the Archbishop of Canterbury to John Paul II: 5 December 1996: 16.

the cause of Catholic–Anglican unity was an imperative. A necessary prerequisite to moving forward theologically was the reception into the lives of both churches of the fruits of what was already agreed.

John Paul II in reply acknowledged the mutual rediscovery of the degree of *real though imperfect communion,* and the new spirit of co-operation in work, prayer and witness that had come about between Anglicans and Catholics. Without expressly saying so, the fact of the ordination of women, for example, caused him to say that 'the path ahead may not be altogether clear to us, but we are here to re-commit ourselves to following it'.[225]

In their *Common Declaration* the Pope and the Archbishop acknowledged that the ordination of women as priests and bishops in some provinces of the Anglican Communion was an obstacle to reconciliation, which they spoke of as 'a new situation'. There was no suggestion of ending the relationship; instead they wrote positively about consulting further and of encouraging ARCIC to continue and to deepen the dialogue.[226]

During vespers and after a commemoration of Saints Gregory the Great and Augustine of Canterbury in the church on the Caelian Hill, the Pope admitted that the ministry of Peter does constitute a difficulty for other Christians. The Archbishop said that it was a cause of sadness that the Sees of Rome and Canterbury are separated. However, any discussion of the Primacy of the Bishop of Rome had a context that included the role of Gregory's successor and an acknowledgment of Anglican roots in the Reformation which 'was not a tragedy so much as a rediscovery'.[227] They signed a *Common Declaration* which we will review in Chapter 6.

225 Address of John Paul II to the Archbishop of Canterbury: 17.
226 *Common Declaration* of John Paul II and Archbishop George Carey, 1996.
227 Address of the Archbishop of Canterbury in the Church of Saints Andrew and Gregory 'al Celio': 5 December 1996: 20.

The New Centre

Entry to the new premises of the Anglican Centre is from the Piazza Collegio Romano, through the large carriage doors that are also the entrance to the Doria Pamphilj gallery. But there was a delay in accessing the new premises because a bankruptcy judge had 'sealed' the rooms. Despite Gesine's application for an injunction against the judge for not completing the liquidation proceedings and releasing the property, it was not until 2 April 1998 that permission was given to proceed with the work. Meantime a preliminary report and plan for the project was drawn up by Sally Thomas, who had already designed St George's College in Jerusalem.

It became very obvious that a second fund-raising programme was needed to refurbish the new premises. William Sanders was appointed appeal director. The earlier estimate of a maximum expenditure of £100,000 was soon replaced by the true cost of £205,000. Archbishop Carey of Canterbury started the ball rolling with an offer of £30,000, suggesting that more could be made available if required. He was asked for a further £50,000. By the end of 1998, £209,000 had been raised.

While the work and the fund-raising were proceeding the Centre had to continue operating. The question was raised about staffing. Vivien, as the administrator, was fulfilling an important role and her salary was increased to match her full-time employment, and it was seen as equally important that Marcella Menna, who had been employed since late 1985 as a secretary, should be offered upgrading, training and a pay increase. She continues today as the librarian and cashier. Carla Farroni, another valuable helper, was housekeeper from early 1984 to September 2005.

The governors asked for an increase in the number of courses offered, including provision for a leaders' course in 1997. The Ruddocks 'felt strongly that they did not have the capacity to arrange this'. Saved by the fact of only a few enquiries, the course was cancelled. The governors proposed instead a 3–4-day course in 1998 'timed to encourage bishops to attend on their way to the Lambeth Conference'. None replied to the personal invitation sent them, so the Ruddocks were able to give time to the relocating. The 1998 Romess summer school, Bruce reported, was a great success with much positive feedback. It was not a matter of religious tourism, but serious thinkers gaining a great deal from the experience.

The librarian of Queen's College, Birmingham, Sheila M. Russell, was called on to assess the Centre's library. Her view was that it was neither well-known nor heavily used. It needed publicity, a more comprehensive and representative stocking, and liaison with other libraries in Rome. The way forward would be 'bound up with the vision which the churches of the Anglican Communion have for an Anglican Centre at the heart of Rome. The *Decree on Ecumenism* of the Second Vatican Council said that the Anglican Communion occupies a "special place" among the Churches separated from the Holy See with roots in the 16th century Reformation. If there is still faith in ecumenism, and that special place is valued, then the recommendations above are a means of carrying forward that vision.'[228]

Relocating and re-establishing the Centre in terms of what was best for it was not an easy job, and this was reflected a little in a tension between the Ruddocks and the Board of Governors. In his very first report to the governors Bruce spoke of 'moments of real despair'[229] in trying to come to terms with the demands of doing a good job; then within six months he identified the great personal cost in trying to re-establish the credibility of the Centre. The governors' response was to acknowledge the quality of Bruce and Vivien's efforts. But they suggested it was time now to move on to the second phase: maintaining the improved quality of relations with the Vatican, being active in the move to the new premises, in raising the profile of the Centre and in the fund-raising.[230] But the Ruddocks observed 'a widening gap between what we are achieving, and the resources to keep going . . . it may well be seen as an example of the Anglican

228 Sheila Russell: Report on the Anglican Centre Library. 5 February 1998.

229 Report by Bruce Ruddock for the meeting of the Governors. 23 November 1995: 1.

230 Minutes of a Meeting of the Governors of the Anglican Centre. 20–21 November 1996: 8.2.

Communion's lack of commitment to Anglican–Roman Catholic relations.' The governors' suggestion of having a course for bishops *en route* to Lambeth was, in Vivien's view, 'a potential last straw'.[231]

Opening of the new Centre

On 12 February 1999 Archbishop George Carey dedicated the new Centre. He remarked that 'the impact of the Second Vatican Council was not limited to the Roman Catholic Church. It greatly stirred other Churches, not least the Anglican Communion.'[232] The outcome was the establishing in 1966 of the Centre with its particular ministry in Rome. The Archbishop recalled that, as a young lecturer and parish man, 'the three weeks I spent here at the Centre changed my entire ecumenical perspective. Two years later I returned to do some independent study on the Virgin Mary – again influenced by the Centre.'[233] Speaking of the work of the Ruddocks, the Archbishop said they had made it a place of warm hospitality.

John Paul II's message was that the Centre is one of the fruits of the rediscovery of Anglican–Catholic brotherhood. He noted the momentum of events, from the Anglican Communion being the first to accept officially the invitation to send observers to the council, to the historic meeting of Pope Paul VI and Archbishop Michael Ramsey. It was during his visit that, 'the Archbishop established the Anglican Centre to be a very visible sign in Rome of the commitment of the whole Anglican Communion to the dialogue that was to be undertaken with the Catholic Church'.[234]

---

231 Report by Bruce Ruddock for the meeting of the Governors. 19 November 1997: 6.
232 'Archbishop of Canterbury's Address at the opening of the new premises of the Anglican Centre in Rome' in *ACR Centro*. June 1999: 8.
233 Ibid.
234 Letter of John Paul II, sent through Cardinal Cassidy, to Archbishop Carey and to Canon and Mrs Bruce Ruddock on the occasion of the dedication of the new Anglican Centre in Rome. 11 February 1999 in *Information Service*: 1999/1: 13–14.

That same day, 12 February 1999, Archbishop Carey presented to Vivien and Bruce the Silver Cross of St Augustine and St George.

Sixth Director: Bishop John Baycroft (September 1999–June 2001)

The significance of John Baycroft's short stay in Rome as the sixth director of the Centre should not be underestimated. First, he was a bishop; second, he was a long-standing member of ARCIC. His appointment was a transition point for the Centre, bringing the official relationship with PCPCU much closer and to a new level. His colleague and friend, Jean Tillard, was involved with ARCIC from the beginning, Baycroft from the time of ARCIC II. They worked together for 17 years, and since Tillard's death John is ARCIC's memory. He knows how the documents were composed and the issues involved.

Bishop Baycroft, a Yorkshire man, was born in Cleveland on 2 June 1933. He resigned as Bishop of Ottawa (1993–9) to become the director of the Centre, a position he filled for the duration of the Jubilee Year. John went home for Christmas 2000, and because of sickness did not return to Rome. There was an interregnum from Christmas 2000 to November 2001 when his successor assumed the directorship.

Within two months of taking up the post, he looked for an administrator for the Centre. Mrs Geraldine Tomlin was appointed to fill the job description he dreamed up, that 'The skipper wants someone with the skills of a chief engineer who is willing to double as the stoker so that the ship is not only afloat but readily responds to the helm.' Geraldine began work on 8 December 1999 and retired in June 2004.

St Peter's 'is part of our home. It helps us feel our rootedness,' he told me when we met in February 2003. Bishop John saw the Centre as an important place for pilgrims. Among his pilgrim guests were the Queen and the Duke of Edinburgh who made an ecumenical visit to the Centre on 17 October 2000 to meet about 30 representatives of Churches in Rome. In May of that

year he welcomed Stuart Burgess, then President of the Methodist Church in Great Britain, Archbishop David Hope of York
and Bishop John Crowley of the Catholic diocese of Middles-
brough, who came together on pilgrimage to Rome. They had
a private audience with the Pope, met with Cardinal Cassidy,
and visited the *Centro pro Unione* and the Anglican Centre.
The three of them talked of their ministry as if it were one thing.
'Rome does that to people,' John said. One morning Stuart and
Archbishop Hope sat in the piazza of St Peter's and, looking
at the basilica, they expressed their hope that the new millennium would bring Christians closer together. On the feast of St
Hendrick, the patron of Finland, the Orthodox, Lutheran and
Catholic bishops visited the Centre on their pilgrimage to Rome.
From Belfast, a Church of Ireland parish and a Roman Catholic
parish called; they asked John about the Centre's mission. 'I
replied "reconciliation".' That word meant a lot to them as they
made their pilgrimage, praying together for reconciliation and
healing in Northern Ireland.

Reflecting on the courses offered, he saw them as having an
important place in the Centre's life.

> Whereas they were formerly for leaders, now they are more
> 'self-select'. A fund exists to help people from poorer Church-
> es to come to programmes here. Their presence builds an
> appreciation of the worldwide scope of Anglicanism. On one
> course there was a Burmese bishop who was asked to pre-
> side at the Eucharist celebrated in a second century catacomb
> using the prayer of Hippolytus. He brought with him a gift
> for the Pope from the Catholic Archbishop in Burma, and so
> we managed to arrange a private audience for him to deliver
> the gift. Making connections, and there are so many of them,
> is part of the Centre's role.

Urgent work required at the Centre

Within days of the Queen's visit in October 2000 there was a
serious collapse in the ceiling of the throne room of the gallery,

immediately below the Centre. Archivists and architects discovered that over the centuries the original fourteenth-century palazzo had been enveloped by a seventeenth-century wing of the present palazzo, and for reasons known only to experts, the floor of the Centre over time was displaced by 7.7 centimetres.

Major reconstruction was a matter of urgency, including attention to both the walls and the floors. It began in late June 2001, lingering on until November 2002. Much of the work happened during the interregnum, so responsibility for keeping the place functioning was in the hands of Geraldine Tomlin.

Seventh Director: Bishop Richard Garrard (October 2001–April 2003)

Bishop Richard Garrard was a worthy successor to Bishop Baycroft, arriving in Rome on 18 October 2001 to take up the position as the seventh director of the Centre. But there was no room at the inn for Dick and his artist wife, Ann. The Centre was still five months away from the completion of the restoration, so they settled for temporary accommodation in an apartment in the Piazza Navona. The day after they arrived they learned that some of their most cherished and irreplaceable possessions had been stolen in England from the loaded and locked van that awaited shipment to Italy. A week later, Ann sprained her ankle. It was as displaced and deprived persons that Ann and Dick initiated their Roman mission. Bishop Garrard retired from the position of suffragan bishop of Penrith to take up this directorship. In those early months he trotted through the narrow streets of ancient Rome, from the Piazza Navona where they were living, to the new Anglican Centre in the Piazza Collegio Romano.

Dick looked closely at what had evolved over the years as the director's 'job description', and he began to question it. There was an understandable emphasis on the place of hospitality and the offering of up to six courses each year, and acting as a bridge between the Anglican Communion and PCPCU, and various other Vatican departments. But he detected an emerging new reality. There was not the same hope as once there had been in Anglican–Catholic relations, reflected in the underuse of the library by students of the Pontifical Universities. Nor was there the same ease of contact with the Vatican, except for relations with the Council for Unity which were always cordial and productive. In a certain sense, the Centre had outlived its usefulness, but this is not to say it is without a future. Both the Anglican Communion and the Vatican needed to think more about what they wanted of the Centre, he told me when we met shortly before the end of his term as director. Being a strong supporter of IARCCUM – the International Anglican–Roman Catholic Commission for Unity and Mission – whose aim is that Anglicans and Catholics should do together 'whatever is possible in the present stage of real but imperfect communion', he asked: why is this not happening in Anglican Centre relations with the Vatican?

It was his mind that the Centre should somehow have involvement in councils, such as Peace and Justice, Migrants and Itinerants, Culture, Christian Unity and Interreligious Dialogue. Archbishop Carey gave some support to Richard's idea, even suggesting it to Cardinal Kasper. One success he did have was involving the Congregation for the Clergy in a ministerial in-service course that he set in place for late 2003. The contribution of the Congregation was by way of a presentation and not an exchange of ideas and principles. 'Our attempts to have an exchange simply met with puzzlement,' he told me.

Working co-operatively with other Churches or institutions was another real possibility. He was aware of the increasing interest among Lutherans following the Augsburg agreement, about having a presence in Rome. Their post-Augsburg feeling, Richard remarked, was a bit like Anglican post-Vatican II feeling. Aware that Anglicans and Lutherans are in communion in virtue of Porvoo, he suggested that they should look at the possibility of working collaboratively in Rome. He also worked on establishing a link with Liverpool Hope University College, which has now become a reality.

Five courses were offered during 2003, four in 2004, five

in 2005 and five in 2006. Jonathan Boardman was the course chaplain, considered essential to the courses. There was a Lenten visitor, Richard noted, when 'our parish priest came to do the Easter blessing of the Centre and our apartment. He looked suitably nervous at dealing with "non-Catholics", so we took him into the chapel and had the prayers there. I gave him €10 as a thank-you.'[235]

Archbishop Carey's Final Visit to Rome

Archbishop Carey's sixth and final official visit to Rome was in June 2002 when he stayed with the British ambassador to the Holy See, visited two councils, and the Anglican exhibition at the Vatican museums. The exhibition *Anglicanism and the Western Christian Tradition: Continuity and Change* was very well done. It traced the history of Christianity in England from the arrival of St Augustine of Canterbury in the sixth century to the present. The initiative to put on the exhibition had come from Her Majesty's Ambassador to the Holy See, Mr Mark Pellew. In correspondence with Stephen Platten, by now Chairman of the Governors of the Anglican Centre and Dean of Norwich, Ambassador Pellew had suggested that an English Cathedral might stage the exhibition and a colloquium in partnership with the Embassy to the Holy See. The practical changes were great both in raising the necessary finance and in negotiating the complex theological and diplomatic hurdles which are unavoidable in relationships at this level between two world communions. The Ambassador and the Dean were joined in organizing the enterprise by the Archdeacon of Norwich, Clifford Offer. The exhibition would not have been possible without the support of Bishop Richard Garrard who offered the use of the Anglican Centre as a 'forward base'. Both the exhibition and the colloquium added a new key element to the dialogue between the churches in terms of mutually understanding each other's histories; the book of the colloquium stands as a continuing

---

235 Richard Garrard: diary entry for 31 March 2003.

record of this initiative. Archbishop Carey was fully supportive and the event offered him the opportunity to make his farewell visit to the Pope, which was a personal conversation and an exchange of messages.

Dr Carey was back in Rome in May of the following year when he gave a paper at the Lateran University. He spoke of both the 'real but imperfect communion' which the Roman Catholic Church has with other churches, and the contemporary and widespread acceptance of *koinonia* or communion as descriptive of the life in Christ that all Christians share, as reasons enough to justify the Pope's desire to share his ministry with other communions. From the viewpoint of the Anglican tradition, the Archbishop asked: 'How might this ministry be exercised even now, in the service of all of us, in tangible forms?' He saw value in the traditional *ad limina* visits to Rome by Catholic bishops from around the world, which prompted the Archbishop to ask if the Pope would consider, from time to time, 'offering informal consultations with church leaders of other Communions'.[236]

A note of pessimism

Despite Archbishop Carey's promotion of the idea of *ad limina* visits to Rome by leaders of other churches, the latter part of John Paul II's pontificate has been assessed negatively by some Anglican commentators. The Archbishop himself, in the speech referred to above, gently suggested that 'the personal ministry of the Bishop of Rome should be clarified, not obscured, by those who serve him in the Curia'. He continued that sometimes 'bureaucracy seems to obscure the clarity of spiritual vision or can even deflect rather than advance it'.[237]

Bishop Garrard sensed a diminishing interest in Anglicans, Protestants and the West generally, alongside an increasing

---

236 Archbishop George Carey, 'Tribute to Pope John Paul II', Rome, May 2003.
237 Ibid.

papal focus on Orthodoxy and the East. Bruce Ruddock, a few years earlier, detected something of the same. He wrote:

> we have become accustomed to the general belief that the relationship between the Roman Catholic Church and the Anglican Church has cooled in recent years, having been side-lined by the Pope's interest in the Eastern Orthodox Church. One has grown used to being told how deeply conservative the Vatican is and how its interest in Anglicanism has diminished. Visitors to the Anglican Centre gaze nostalgically at our photographs of Popes embracing Archbishops of Canterbury and ask where that goodwill has gone.

Bishop Mark Santer, former Chairman of the Anglican Centre, preached on 22 November 1995 at the service of welcome for Bruce and Vivien Ruddock. He mentioned the image of the two lungs – that image of complementarity of Eastern and Western Christianity that has come to the fore in recent years. He said it is a fine image, as long as it is not used to 'make those of us who are heirs to the Protestant Reformation of Northern Europe sometimes wonder whether any place is envisaged for us in the living organism of the Church'.[238]

Stephen Platten's assessment was that 'Anglicans and Roman Catholics have particular cause for pessimism. The 1991 Response of the Holy See to ARCIC I was discouraging, and the decision of the Church of England to ordain women to the priesthood has further dampened ecumenical hopes.' He went on to say that placing these factors within the context of the Vatican's increasing theological and ecclesiological conservatism signals 'greater foreboding in our contemporary world'.[239]

---

238 Mark Santer, 'Address at the service to welcome Bruce and Vivien Ruddock to the Anglican Centre, in the Church of San Marcello al Corso, Rome' *ACR Centro:* January 1996: 2.
239 Stephen Platten, 'Convergence on Morals?' *ACR Centro*: October 1995: 1.

Archbishop Rowan Williams and Two Popes

John Paul II expressed his gratitude to Archbishop Williams (2002–) for visiting him on 4 October 2003, so soon after taking up his new ministry. The Archbishop reaffirmed his commitment to the full, visible unity of the Church, and expressed his gratitude for the work of ARCIC and his hopes for the future through the efforts of IARCCUM.[240] But the Pope spoke of 'new and serious' difficulties that 'have arisen on the path to unity', remarks made in the light of recent events in North America. Alongside the ordination of women, these two events stand in the way of Catholic recognition of Anglican orders.

Nevertheless, Cardinal Kasper, when he spoke at the dinner of welcome to Archbishop Williams on 3 October 2003, stated an important ecumenical principle, that 'precisely when there are problems there is ever greater need of dialogue'.[241] At the installation of Bishop John Flack as the new Director of the Anglican Centre, the Cardinal acknowledged that present-day relations are 'characterized by factors both constructive and problematic'. Then he sounded a very optimistic note: 'let us proceed on the difficult but exhilarating path towards the full visible unity of the Church with a boundless trust in the Lord'.[242]

Archbishop Williams, in reply to the Cardinal, said: 'I cannot pretend that we are not at a testing time at present.' He explained that the questions facing the Anglican Communion, and therefore her ecumenical partners, are not just about contemporary morality but also about the nature of ecclesial communion. He concluded his address on a positive note, saying: 'in the last three years we have redoubled our dialogue, so that we are

---

240 Summaries of the addresses of John Paul II and Archbishop Williams can be found in *ACR Centro:* Advent 2003.
241 Words of welcome to Archbishop Williams by Cardinal Kasper, Dinner at *Domus Sancta Marthae, 3* October 2003.
242 Address of Cardinal Kasper at the Installation of the new Director of the Anglican Centre, Bishop John Flack, *Santa Maria Sopra Minerva,* 4 October 2003.

looking not only for theological convergence but also for the practical outworking of the communion that we share'.[243] He was referring to the twin works of ARCIC and IARCCUM.

Archbishop Rowan Williams

Born in Swansea in 1950, Rowan Williams was raised in a Presbyterian family. In his youth his family began practising in an Anglican parish where Rowan soon developed a love of the liturgy and the Book of Common Prayer. Educated at Cambridge, he researched at Oxford, becoming the Lady Margaret Professor of Divinity from 1986 to 1992, marrying Jane Paul, a lecturer in theology. They have two children. He was Bishop of Monmouth from 1992, then Archbishop of Wales before becoming the Archbishop of Canterbury in 2000. The Archbishop is a highly respected theologian and writer.

Ever grateful to Catholic religious orders, especially the Benedictines and the Dominicans from whom he received stimulation in prayer and theology, he early on was attracted to being a Catholic. Asked by Charles Moore why he did not become a Catholic, he gave two reasons. The first was that he could not bring himself to believe in papal infallibility and the universal ordinary jurisdiction of the Pope. It was not the Church he came to know through studying the Fathers, the Archbishop said. Second, he had reservations about the traditional Catholic doctrine of grace and merit.[244]

He assumed office at a difficult and crucial time in the life of the Communion. Nevertheless, his strong and clear understanding of the nature of unity, and the words he has spoken about it, are more than a hint that this is an important priority for him – 'Unity becomes finally unintelligible and unworthwhile when it itself ceases to be a theological category.' He continues: 'Stay-

---

243 Address in reply of Archbishop Williams, *Sancta Maria Sopra Minerva,* 4 October 2003.
244 Charles Moore interviews the Archbishop of Canterbury: 12 February 2003: www.telegraph.co.uk

ing together is pointless unless it is staying together because of the Body of Christ.'[245]

Archbishop Williams and Benedict XVI

Just a year and a half after his first official visit to Rome, Archbishop Williams returned in April 2005 for the funeral of John Paul II. He wore the pectoral cross that the Pope had presented to him at the time of his appointment to Canterbury, and the ring given to Archbishop Ramsey by Paul VI. Archbishop Williams saw an ecumenical connection between the sickness and death of John Paul II and the beginnings of Pope Benedict's service in the Petrine ministry. The reaction to the death was not just among Catholics, but from people of all denominations, showing 'a kind of foretaste of a worldwide fellowship of people gathered for worship in a way that has somehow gone around the difficulties of doctrinal definition. It is as if we have been given a glimpse of other levels of unity, and my own feeling is that is the level at which he will seek to work'[246] – referring to Benedict XVI.

From the outset of his new ministry Benedict XVI indicated that working for unity was a 'primary commitment', which prompted Margaret Hebblethwaite's assessment that 'his most extravagant commitment is his pledge on ecumenism'.[247] If the Archbishop is correct that Benedict XVI is opting for a broader highway on which we can more comfortably travel the journey to unity then one would expect the Pope's words to be a signpost pointing the way.

In the first major address of his pontificate to the cardinals on the day after his election (19 April) Benedict identified the restoration of full visible unity as an imperative. He said that manifestations of good sentiments are not enough. 'There must be concrete gestures that penetrate spirits and move consciences,

---

245 BBC News UK Edition: 15 October 2003: bbc.co.uk
246 'In the Footsteps of Benedict', *The Tablet* 30 April 2005: 2.
247 'The reconciler reaches out'. *The Tablet* 30 April 2005: 6–7.

leading each one to that interior conversion which is the basis for all progress on the road to ecumenism.' He confirmed the Catholic Church's 'irreversible' commitment to ecumenism and listed three practical steps, already well-known in ecumenical circles: (1) necessity of theological dialogue, (2) in-depth knowledge of the historical reasons of choices made in the past, (3) purification of memories. He pledged to cultivate appropriate contacts and understanding with the different churches and ecclesial communities.

In his homily for the inauguration of his pontificate on 24 April, Benedict XVI spoke of the communion of saints as the 'baptized . . . who draw life from the gift of Christ's Body and Blood'. He then used two symbols, the pallium and the fisherman's ring, both of which 'issue an explicit call to unity'.'The day following, in addressing the leaders of the Christian Churches, Benedict said that the ecumenical objective 'implies a true docility to what the Spirit says to the Churches, courage, gentleness, firmness and hope, in order to reach our goal'. He concluded by calling for a 'spiritual ecumenism, which through prayer, can bring about our communion without obstacles'. [248] At his first public audience on 27 April he described this spiritual ecumenism in the words of the Rule of St Benedict: *Prefer nothing to the love of Christ.*[249] His prayer is that through the intercession of St Benedict, Christ will always have pride of place in our thoughts and in all our actions. When he presided at Vespers at St Paul's Outside-the-Walls on the final day of the Week of Prayer for Christian unity he made reference to his encyclical, promulgated that morning of 25 January 2006, saying 'God is love. On this solid rock the entire faith of the Church is based.'

In this encyclical, which takes its title *Deus Caritas Est* from 1 John 4.16, he is restating the tone for his pontificate which he

---

248 Address of Benedict XVI to the Delegates of other Churches and Ecclesial Communities and of other Religious Traditions. Clementine Hall, 25 April 2005.
249 Rule of St Benedict 72, 11.

first announced when quoting St Benedict's rule. He intends a mission of loving service to all Christians.

The night of the papal inauguration Archbishop Williams also stressed the importance of the centrality of Christ when he preached in All Saints' Church, using John 14, 1–12: 'in my Father's house there are many mansions'.

> Now and then, the Church reveals itself in its fullness, uncovering itself, as in the great acts we have shared. The events of the past weeks have drawn Christians of many traditions together in the sure knowledge that the dwelling-place to which they all belong is Christ, despite the differences among them. With Christ and with one another, the relationship is a living one. The journey to the Father's house, as individuals and as churches, is so vast that we are always journeying into it. As we reach each stopping-place we are challenged to enter into communion with others so as to view together the horizon, realizing that there is more to discover as we move on. Teresa of Avila spoke of moving from level to level, from room to room, to the one at the centre. If we stop, she said, we fall back. There's only one way, to move forward.
>
> We have heard the promise and commitment of Pope Benedict. But what will it bring? The gospel gives the answer – our journey is to Christ's home. We have to trust Christ; we have to trust one another. We have reason to trust one another.[250]

It is very encouraging if the Pope and the Archbishop are thinking the same thoughts and expressing the same sentiments. Time will tell. Behind the beginnings of the pontificate are the several and sometimes prolonged hesitations of the CDF over the ARCIC agreements. There is *Dominus Jesus*, with which Cardinal Ratzinger was so closely associated. It is spoken of as reversing ecumenical gains and as casting a shadow over the papacy. Maybe the Archbishop is right. At this early point in the exercise of the Petrine ministry, and at this stage of the ecumenical journey, Benedict is discovering in a fresh way the breadth

---

250 The Archbishop did not use a script. Notes taken by the author.

of the Church. He is touched by Christian friendships long in the making and the levels of communion already in place. He experienced the great embrace of the Christian world upon his entry into his new ministry. For the sake of all of us he cannot let go of it.

Pope Benedict XVI

Joseph Ratzinger was born on 16 April 1927 and ordained priest with his brother Georg on 29 June 1951. He earned a doctorate on Augustine's doctrine of the Church and spent much of his early life teaching in the universities of Bonn, Münster, Tübingen and Regensburg. His experience as a *peritus* at all the sessions of the Vatican Council, and the scholars he associated with, including Hans Küng, Hans Urs Von Balthasar and Henri de Lubac, as well as a wide range of Protestant theologians, exposed him to the breadth and depth of the Church. Joseph Ratzinger became Archbishop of Munich and Freising in 1977 and Cardinal of Munich the same year. Called to Rome, he became Prefect of the CDF for 24 years, his successor being Archbishop William Levada of the United States.

Elected Bishop of Rome on 19 April 2005, the oldest in 275 years, he chose the name of Benedict XVI. Within days of the start of his work he referred to the strong historic link between the Rule of St Benedict and England. It is the land to which Pope Gregory the Great sent Benedictine monks to establish the Church and where Benedictine monasticism has played an important part in the development of the Church.

Eighth Director: Bishop John Flack (2003–)

Archbishop Williams installed Bishop Flack as the eighth Director of the Centre in October 2003. Santa Maria sopra Minerva, the titular church of Cardinal Murphy-O'Connor, the Archbishop of Westminster, was packed for the evening prayer service. Cardinal Murphy-O'Connor and Cardinal Walter Kasper were present.

John was born in 1942 and educated at the University of Leeds and the College of the Resurrection, Mirfield. Ordained in 1967, his ministry has been mainly as a parish priest in industrial Yorkshire, then Archdeacon of Pontefract from 1992 and Bishop of Huntingdon since 1997. He is married to Julia, a Senior Probation Officer at Peterborough, and they have two children. A keen Yorkshire League cricketer in days past, John plays the piano and the organ, and is particularly interested in the music of Mozart. He is in Rome on a four-year appointment, and feels very comfortable and confident in this post after long and harmonious relations with Catholic priests in his various pastoral appointments.

I asked Bishop Flack about his vision for the Centre. He made four points. In the first place, he said, he wants the Centre to be a place of dialogue for leaders from both communions and for clergy, laity and particularly for students from Roman universities and from religious orders. He hopes the Centre will become a place for deep study of divisive matters such as the Petrine ministry, the ordination of women and some of the ethical issues. Above all, he wants the Centre to help give people a 'heart' for ecumenism, in line with Cardinal Newman's words *cor ad cor loquitor*. A second aim is for the Centre to foster the study of theology in all its aspects. Liverpool Hope University, an ecumenical college, and the Centre jointly promote an ecumenism module of two weeks each year. The participating students have a one-week experience of Rome and the other week at Liverpool Hope, credit being earned towards a Master's degree.[251] The Centre is particularly keen to have students from Roman universities using its facilities, and to this end the library is now on-line at www.anglicancentreinrome.org.

The third goal relates to the weeklong courses that have been offered for many years, the intention now is to open them up to

_____

251 Liverpool Hope University is an amalgamation of two Roman Catholic colleges, Notre Dame and Christ's, and an Anglican college, St Katharine's. It is now an ecumenical college of over 7000 students and 700 staff.

all Christians, lay as well as ordained. Thus the Centre wishes to see itself as a place for life-long learning for all within the Church. The Board of Studies has been enlarged to five members, reflecting the Centre's determination to offer the highest standard of teaching. Five courses will be offered during 2007:

(1) Benedictine Spirituality, led by Canon Peter Sills of Ely Cathedral.
(2) Why study the Old Testament? led by Visiting Fellow Dr Bill Franklin.
(3) Anglican/Roman Catholic Ecumenism led by the staff of Liverpool Hope University and the Rome Anglican Centre.
(4) Rome – life and death in the eternal city, led by the Anglican Centre staff.
(5) Is there a future for Anglican Christianity? led by Professor Stephen Sykes.

Finally, hospitality remains an important feature of the Centre: all genuine enquirers are welcomed, the doors open from 9.00 a.m. to 5.00 p.m. Monday to Friday when a member of staff is always on duty. The overnight facilities have been upgraded, and every Tuesday there is an open Eucharist in the newly designed chapel, followed by lunch for everyone.

As from 1 July 2005 Sara MacVane, a Deacon on the staff of All Saints', became half-time assistant to the Director at the Centre. In September 2005 Dr Bill Franklin, a Visiting Fellow, began a three-year appointment in Rome, working at the American Academy and also at the Anglican Centre where he is upgrading the library. Grace Jones has taken up the position of Lay Ministry Adviser and is also responsible for the Centre website.

The Future

Has the Anglican Centre a future?

It is so easy to wonder about the Anglican Centre's future in virtue of the number of problems that earlier beset it. There was the seemingly never-ending financial difficulty, and the deflation that soon followed the post-Vatican II enthusiasm for reunion that once appeared to be just down the road. There is also the search for an appropriate relationship with the Holy See, beyond being 'around' to respond to ceremonial moments when invited. Then, there is the distancing that has occurred, on the one hand because of the Vatican Curia's inability to enter into the ecumenical way of doing things and on the other the Anglican departure from the long-standing Christian tradition of a male-only priesthood.

The Anglican Centre has in fact weathered the financial storm, and is now securely placed. A competent board of directors is supervising sound investments and appropriate management of resources. The Centre is by no means over-endowed and could well benefit from some generous benefactions to ensure its future. As far as working relations with the Vatican are concerned, these are more than cordial. Nevertheless, openness to possibilities in light of the Lund Principle – first enunciated over 50 years ago – is not an unreasonable request to make. It says that 'Churches ask themselves . . . whether they should not act together in all matters except those in which deep differences in conviction compel them to act separately'. Bishop Mark Santer, as the delegate of the Anglican Communion at the Special Assembly for Europe of the Synod of Bishops in 1991, expressed sorrow at the fact that when working in small groups 'the fraternal delegates will be by themselves and not with the Catholic Bishops of their own language group'. He continued: 'If we are really to exchange our experience, our hopes and our fears, we must talk to one another and not only about one another.'[252]

Finally, the presence of the Centre, no matter what the current difficulties happen to be, is a signpost that visible unity remains the goal. With Archbishop Rowan Williams in Canterbury and Pope Benedict XVI in Rome we pray confidently for a secure

---

252 'Address by Bishop Mark Santer, Delegate of the Anglican Communion, to the European Synod of Bishops' *L'OR* 4 December 1991: 4.

and lasting relationship between the two Churches and an increasingly important role for the Anglican Centre.

The future of the Anglican–Roman Catholic dialogue

We have passed beyond the days of ecumenical optimism when Anglicans and Catholics felt corporate reunion was just around the corner. This optimism revived when there was talk of Catholic recognition of Anglican Orders, given the development of the 'new context'. Then came the ordination of women to the priesthood and the episcopate in some provinces of the Anglican Communion, the consecration of Bishop Gene Robinson in the United States and the approval of a Public Rite of Blessing for same-sex unions in Canada.

These developments have altered the ecumenical relationship of the two Churches. The Catholic Church sees these actions within the Anglican Communion as obstacles in the way of full corporate reunion, so much so that the path towards this goal is no longer clear. Nevertheless, it is important to continue the theological dialogue. ARCIC III is likely to commence in 2007.

Over and above the formal theological dialogue, Cardinal Kasper suggests an additional way of relating. Pointing to the New Testament Church, he identifies a 'unity in the diversity of charisms, offices, local churches and cultures. Unity is symphonic; unity is *communion sanctorum*, that is, shared participation in the holy, in the life of God, in the Holy Spirit, in the Gospel, in the one baptism, and in the one Eucharistic body of the Lord.'[253] Given this scriptural model of ecclesial unity in diversity, it is perfectly reasonable for Christians to seek the same today. He continues 'that every Church has elements of the gospel, elements of ecclesiality'. What is especially significant is his observation that various churches beyond the bounds of the Catholic Church may have 'developed these elements profounder and deeper and larger that we have done'. He is

---

253 Pat Ashworth, 'Unity is symphonic, says Cardinal' in *Church Times* 27 January 2006.

referring, among other things, to the importance given to the Word of God and to preaching.

Anglican Bishop Tom Wright of Durham, who was attending the same colloquium as Cardinal Kasper at Durham University, 12–17 January 2006, noted the Cardinal's slant, and interprets it this way:

> There are very serious voices within the Roman Catholic Church saying we are not three or four different Churches; we are all part of the one single Church which has some serious internal problems to be addressed. That's a very different way of stating the ecumenical jigsaw than we have been used to. The notion of Rome asking itself, 'What can we as Rome receive as gifts from other Churches in order that we can be more complete?' is so different from the impression that has sometimes been given of Churches thinking they basically have everything and it's other Churches who need to learn from them.[254]

This 'new way' has been given a name – 'Receptive Ecumenism'. It happens when a Church sets out, not primarily to teach others, but to receive from others. The way of receptive ecumenism should have appeal to Anglicans and Catholics.

---

254 Ibid

6

Anglicans and Catholics in Dialogue

What Shall We Make of ARCIC and IARCCUM?

The modern story of Anglicans in Rome began with the April 1961 arrival of Bernard Pawley as the representative of the Archbishops of Canterbury and York to the Holy See. From 1962 through 1965 Anglicans were in Rome to observe but, more than that, they came to contribute to the evolving work of the Vatican Council. Since then, Archbishops of Canterbury have been constant visitors to the eternal city, alongside a host of Anglican pilgrims from throughout the Communion. The Directors of the Anglican Centre have maintained a steady role, reminding the Catholic Church of Anglicanism's rich heritage, and providing a presence that Rome is learning that it cannot do without. Then, there are the two parishes of All Saints' and St Paul's Within-the-Walls which minister to local and visiting Anglicans and Episcopalians, and have an effective outreach in the community.

When the Vatican Council came to a close it was realized that another line of contact needed to be put in place, and it was to initiate dialogue between the two Communions. Scholars were enlisted, Catholic and Anglican, to name the historical and theological features that the two Communions had continued to hold in common, to surface the issues where they diverged, and to study the paths leading to the fullness of unity. The forum in which this would happen was named the Anglican Roman Catholic International Commission, or ARCIC.

This book would be incomplete if attention were not given to the ARCIC story. It is a long story and most of us can become confused by the vast array of meetings that have occurred and statements that have been published, and at what is likely to happen next. The intention, therefore, is to take a straightforward approach, by identifying the sequence of events which make up ARCIC I (1970–82), occasionally offering comment, and following the same procedure in considering ARCIC II (1983–2005), and after that, IARCCUM. Beyond what is said here the reader will find a wide range of material written on ARCIC and its many statements.

ARCIC I

The Common Declaration

Two days after dedicating the Rome Anglican Centre in March 1966, Archbishop Ramsey had a historic and memorable meeting with Pope Paul VI in the Basilica of St Paul Outside-the-Walls. They signed the *Common Declaration*, thereby launching the serious dialogue 'founded on the Gospels and on the ancient common traditions',[255] which soon would become known as ARCIC.

The Joint Preparatory Commission and its Malta Report

There was rapid follow-up to the signing of the *Common Declaration*. In May of that year, 1966, Bishop Willebrands was at Lambeth discussing the procedures for establishing a Joint Preparatory Commission. In June, Anglican Bishop John Moorman and Catholic Bishop Charles Helmsing were appointed co-chairmen. Meeting first in January of 1967, the last of three very busy consultations was in January of 1968, when *The Malta Report*[256] came to light.

---

255 'The Common Declaration by Pope Paul VI and the Archbishop of Canterbury' in *The Final Report*, CTS/SPCK, 1982: 117–18.
256 'Report of the Anglican–Roman Catholic Joint Preparatory Commission' (*The Malta Report*) in *The Final Report*, CTS/SPCK, 1982: 108–16.

Its principal recommendation was to establish a *Permanent Joint Commission*, the word 'Permanent' in the title later replaced by 'International' so as not to give the impression that the separation of the two Communions was necessarily permanent. The report spoke of the common faith, the common baptism in the one Church, the shared scriptures, creeds and teachings of the Fathers, and the rich inheritance in liturgy, theology, spirituality, Church order and mission. The divergences arising since the sixteenth century are 'not so much from the substance of this inheritance as from our separate way of receiving it'.[257] Further study would surface those differences that needed serious investigation, and matters of possible convergence. Particular recommendations for dialogue included intercommunion, certain doctrines of the Church, such as the Mariological definitions, ministry and authority, including the Petrine primacy and infallibility and the legislation on mixed marriages. *The Malta Report* also offered practical suggestions ranging from annual joint meetings of the hierarchy to pulpit exchanges and prayer in common.

The *Report* was submitted to the Pope and the Archbishop soon after the completion of the Malta meeting in January 1968. The hope was that responses would be forthcoming in time for the Lambeth Conference of that same year. All the responses from the Anglican metropolitans were to hand by 1 April, but even by the end of the Lambeth Conference the Catholic episcopal conferences had still not seen it. The CDF withheld permission for it to be sent out, despite the fact that the report had been distributed during the recently concluded Lambeth Conference, and therefore was public. *The Tablet* printed it on 31 November as did the *National Catholic Reporter* at an earlier date.

William Purdy, an officer of the SPCU and also one of the secretaries of the Joint Preparatory Commission, was close to the scene and shared the frustration imposed by the Roman offices. He spoke of a 'gulf between the Secretariat's (and still

---

257 *The Malta Report* n 4.

more the Joint Preparatory Commission's) conception of the nature and importance of its task and that of the Secretariat of State and the Congregation for the Doctrine of the Faith, and the contrast of both mind and feeling which they brought to reading the report'.[258] It never received official endorsement from Catholic authorities. Nevertheless, the process had begun and there was no stopping it.

The Permanent Joint Commission

The first meeting of the recommended *Permanent Joint Commission* was at Windsor in England, beginning on 9 January 1970. It was here that the word 'International' replaced 'Permanent', thus giving rise to the acronym ARCIC – *The Anglican Roman Catholic International Commission*. The co-chairmen were Anglican Bishop Henry McAdoo (later Archbishop of Dublin, from 1977) and Catholic Bishop Alan Clark, with eight theologians and one co-secretary on each team. Christopher Hill points out that the Anglican members were English or of English origin, with nobody from black African or Asian Anglicanism. It was also underrepresentative of evangelicals, and no women were part of the team. The Catholic representatives comprised English, French and North Americans.[259]

One can understand that it would take time for such a new venture between the two Communions to come up with an appropriate dialogue method. At this very early stage the method decided upon was the presentation of joint papers. Bishop Edward Knapp-Fisher and Father Edmund Hill OP presented on the fundamentals of faith under these headings: Revelation and faith, Scripture and Tradition, Church and authority.

---

258 William Purdy, *The Search for Unity: Relations Between the Anglican and Roman Catholic Churches From the 1950's to the 1970's*, London: Geoffrey Chapman, 1996: 112.
259 Michael Hill, 'ARCIC I and II. An Anglican Perspective'. A paper presented in Malines, 31 August 1996. It was delivered again at the Annual General Meeting of the Ecumenical Society of the Blessed Virgin Mary on 7 March 1998, and printed in their bulletin: 4.

Bishop Vogel and Father Jean-Marie Tillard OP examined the matter of intercommunion and the related topics of Church and ministry. Bishop Butler and Professor Henry Chadwick spoke on authority, its nature, exercise and implications.

Very much an exploratory meeting, the agenda proposed in *The Malta Report* was modified so as to create an opportunity to establish the extent to which the two communions share the same faith on Eucharist, Ministry and Ordination, and Authority. Thus, sub-committees, determined geographically with an eye to convenience in the follow-up work, considered the three topics, offering some preliminary responses at a meeting in Venice, September 1970. Thereafter, ARCIC would work on these three subjects one by one, as we shall soon discover.

One further word before we turn to each of the three subjects is to mention the evolution of the 'ecumenical method'. Having theoretically moved from standing in judgement on one another, the two communions picked up on the idea that together they needed to deepen their understanding of the scriptures and the early traditions. They were prompted into thinking along these lines by a number of movements that were at work in the decades of the first half of the twentieth century. These were the biblical movement, the patristic movement and the liturgical movement, all having something important to say.[260] The combined impact of the emerging scholarship from them was that the two communions would benefit immensely by jointly returning to their shared origin, and moving on from there. This method was given endorsement in the earlier cited 1966 *Common Declaration* which said that the Pope and the Archbishop 'intend to inaugurate between the Roman Catholic Church and the Anglican Communion a serious dialogue which, founded on the Gospels and on the ancient common traditions, may lead to that unity in truth, for which Christ prayed'.[261] As

---

260 See Frederick M. Bliss, *Catholic and Ecumenical: History and Hope*, Franklin: Sheed and Ward, 1999: 40–44 for a review of the work of these movements.
261 *The Common Declaration*: 118.

Christopher Hill observed, ARCIC did follow this method, very rarely setting confessional positions side by side. Even when discussing the Vatican I understanding of the universal ministry of the Bishop of Rome, their statement was made jointly.[262]

As a result of patristic scholarship, for instance, the word *koinonia* or 'communion' appeared, which Cardinal Murphy-O'Connor speaks of as the key to understanding ARCIC. The 'relationship with each other, *koinonia*, communion, is the Church. It is because we are in real communion, *koinonia*, with each other that we are able to dialogue, to speak about the Church and to grow in things that are fundamental to its reality.'[263] The key for ARCIC is that this *koinonia* is grounded in our *koinonia* in the life of the Trinity.

In his first meeting with ARCIC at Castel Gandolfo in September 1980, John Paul II made a very interesting statement, his words worthy of quote:

> Your method has been to go behind the habit of thought and expression born and nourished in enmity and controversy, to scrutinise together the great common treasure, to clothe it in a language at once traditional and expressive of the insights of an age which no longer glories in strife but seeks to come together in listening to the quiet voice of the Spirit.[264]

The reason why we have 'stayed' with this topic of 'method' is because understanding something about it is a necessary prerequisite to appreciating and assessing ecumenical statements. Not only individuals need to have this understanding, so also do the officials of the receiving Churches.

---

262 Christopher Hill, 'ARCIC I and II. An Anglican Perspective'. Talk given to the Ecumenical Society of the Blessed Virgin, 7 March 1998: 6.
263 Cardinal Cormac Murphy-O'Connor, 'The Work of ARCIC 1968–2000' in *One in Christ*, January 2004: 24–5.
264 'The way past the Vatican roadblock', in *The Tablet* 16 January 1992: 59–60.

Eucharist: Windsor 1971 and Elucidation 1979

Since the Eucharist is so intimately tied to the Church's identity it was judged important to establish at the outset the level of eucharistic agreement between the two communions. The regular practice of the Commission was to publish its statement and then to invite comment and criticism. Once the comments were received, and in the light of them, an *Elucidation* or explanation would be prepared and published, usually some years later.

It was inevitable that the Commission would have to address two long-standing areas of controversy in eucharistic theology and belief – Sacrifice and Presence. Regarding the first, the Catholic understanding of the 'Sacrifice of the Mass' seemed to Anglicans a denial of the sufficiency of Christ's death on Calvary, a once-only sacrifice which cannot be repeated. But, thanks to the insights arising out of the biblical movement, the language of *anamnesis* or 'remembering', which the Church does liturgically, means that the past *is made present*, or *is remembered*, according to the richest biblical understanding of that word 'remembered'. By the action of the Holy Spirit the present-day believer is inserted into Christ's sacrifice, in such a way that the Eucharist is rightly understood as the sacrifice of Christ.

The second point, the Real Presence of Christ in the Eucharist, developed controversially mainly because of the Catholic insistence on speaking of 'transubstantiation' as the one and only way of explaining the change in the inner reality of the bread and wine becoming the body and blood of Christ. ARCIC's choice was to strongly affirm the fact of the radical change effecting the real presence, but setting the explanation in the context of the ultimate purpose of the Eucharist, a presence brought about through the action of the Holy Spirit for the believer. The word 'transubstantiation', though neither included in the text as such, nor repudiated by ARCIC, is included by way of a footnote.

So satisfied were the members of the Commission at the level of consensus achieved that, in the *Elucidations* eight years later, they said their 'document represents not only the judgement of all its members – i.e. it is an agreement – but their unanimous agreement on essential matters where it considers that doctrine admits no divergence i.e. it is a substantial agreement'.[265] This was a very important 'first' in the ARCIC story.

Ministry and Ordination: Canterbury 1973 and Elucidation 1979

The Preface to the statement on Ministry and Ordination indicates the status ascribed to the document by the Commission: 'that in what we have said here both Anglicans and Roman Catholics will recognize their own faith'. It begins by identifying the priesthood of the faithful which arises from baptism, as the context within which the ordained ministry finds its 'particular sacramental relationship with Christ as High Priest'.[266] The ordained are to serve the faithful who are to serve the wider community.

Agreement was considered as a necessary prerequisite to any discussion of Leo XIII's 1896 judgement on the validity of Anglican orders. This contemporary development in thinking about the nature of the Church and the work of ARCIC on the doctrine of ministry placed the question of orders in a 'new context', which John Paul II and Archbishop Runcie acknowledged in their 1982 *Common Declaration*. They instructed the new International Commission to study 'all that hinders mutual recognition of the ministries of our Communions'.[267] Subsequently, Cardinal Willebrands wrote encouragingly to the co-chairmen of ARCIC on the desirability of a new evaluation by the Catholic Church on the rites currently used in Anglican ordinations. The co-chairmen in their reply spoke both of the 'ARCIC process' offering a way forward, and of the ordination of women in some parts of the Anglican Communion creating a major difficulty.[268] The problem was subsequently further compounded by an altogether different matter, the episcopal

---

265 'Elucidation' in Final Report n 2: 17.
266 'Elucidation' in Final Report n 2: 41.
267 'Common Declaration' n 3.
268 'Anglican Orders. A New Context', London: Catholic Truth Society, 1986.

consecration of the actively gay bishop in the United States. How the Anglican Communion will respond to this situation is a second factor that will affect the goal of the reconciliation of ministries in the future.

Authority in the Church I: Venice 1976 and Elucidation 1981

The beginnings of the Church of England involved a repudiation of papal jurisdiction and the adoption of what has turned out to be a highly dispersed style of authority in the Anglican Communion. The two communions, therefore, went their separate ways, made all the more obvious with the 1870 conciliar definitions of papal primacy and infallibility, indicative of an ever-increasing level of centralization in the Catholic Church. The starting point chosen, therefore, was not in any debate of matters of controversy, but in a study of the nature of authority and its contribution to a shaping of the Church.

The identification of the primary authority of scripture and the role of the Holy Spirit in safeguarding the revelation of Jesus Christ laid the foundations. Following logically, there came a study of the historic emergence of the episcopacy and of conciliar life in the Church, and inevitably recognition of the vocabulary of ecclesial authority, including indefectibility, infallibility, inerrancy, reception and the *sensus fidelium*.

It would be unrealistic to expect the Commission to present its report using a term such as 'substantial agreement', as was the case with the Eucharist document. Instead *Authority I* speaks of 'the consensus we have reached' and 'our degree of agreement' (Introduction), though the document concludes that the Statement 'represents a significant convergence'. Such is a tribute to the wisdom of the delegates that they first chose to lay appropriate foundations that brought them to this particular point of consensus. They concluded their study, naming a number of problem issues that would become the agenda for *Authority II,* namely the Petrine texts, the 'divine right' of the papacy, jurisdiction and finally the infallibility of the Pope.

Authority in the Church II: Windsor 1981

As a prelude to their examination of the four problem areas related to the primacy, the Commission acknowledged that many of the 'Petrine texts' witness to an early tradition that Peter was called by Jesus to a special role. This call, during the ministry of Jesus, gave Peter responsibility for strengthening the brethren and overcoming threats to the Church's unity (n 5). It becomes problematic in that there is a lack of any explicit biblical statement about the transmission of Peter's leadership role and a lack of clarity about the transmission of apostolic authority. Yet the Church of Rome and its bishop were recognized very early on 'as possessing a unique responsibility among the churches . . . and a special service in relation to the unity of the churches' (n 6). Given this background, the Commission felt comfortable enough to conclude that

> If the leadership of the bishop of Rome has been rejected by those who thought it was not faithful to the truth of the Gospel and hence not a true focus of unity, we nevertheless agree that a universal primacy will be needed in a reunited Church and should appropriately be the primacy of the bishop of Rome. (n 9)

In considering the second problem, the Commission begins with two explicit questions: What does *ius divinum* or 'divine right' mean with respect to the Roman primacy, and, what are the implications for the ecclesial status of non-Catholic communions (n 10)?

The answer to the first has to do with God's purpose for the Church. The primate or Bishop of Rome – by right – is the sign within the universal college of bishops of the visible *koinonia* of the whole Church, and as such is an instrument through which unity in diversity is realized (n 11). Such is essentially a Catholic answer which Anglicans, given improving relations, also accept but with one proviso, that the primacy is understood not so much as a 'right' but as 'a gift of divine providence' (n 13). The answer to the second rests in the Second Vatican Council's teaching that ecclesial or Church identity is no longer an exclusively Catholic characteristic, but belongs in Anglican and in other communities as well. The outcome is that 'the primacy of the bishop of Rome can be affirmed as part of God's design for the universal *koinonia* in terms which are compatible with both our traditions' (n 15).

The third problem is about the meaning of jurisdiction, in particular the declaration of *Pastor Aeternus* that the Lord gave to Peter true and proper jurisdiction and not just a position of honour. The immediate impact of the language used by Vatican I – that the jurisdiction is universal, ordinary and immediate – is somewhat off-putting and as *Authority II* says 'has aggravated the difficulties'. It is helpful to realize that since there is a number of offices and functions within the Church, all of which serve the *koinonia*, the distribution of authority will match the precise needs that are being served, be they diocesan, metropolitan or universal. The Bishop of Rome as the universal primate, in virtue of his office, receives and exercises ordinary and immediate jurisdiction and does so universally because he is charged with the responsibility of serving the entire communion. As n 21 says, 'The purpose of the universal primate's jurisdiction is to enable him to further catholicity as well as unity and to foster and draw together the riches of the diverse traditions of the churches.' Herein rests an important assurance.

Infallibility is the final problem. It is agreed that doctrinal decisions must match the community's faith 'as grounded in Scripture and interpreted by the mind of the Church', but there is a question: can one person enjoy 'a special ministerial gift of discerning the truth and of teaching' (n 23)? The answer is 'yes', though there is a point of difference between Catholic and Anglican thinking on one particular aspect of the process. It is that Anglicans do not accept the term 'infallibility' which is understood by Catholics to mean that the bishop of Rome enjoys a guaranteed gift of divine assistance when making such judgements. Certainty, for Anglicans, will be indicated by means of a subsequent reception process among the faithful.

Final Report: 1981

The Commission was requested by Canterbury and Rome to complete its work, which it did by bringing together all the above Reports and Elucidations, and publishing them in 1981 as the *Final Report*. The co-chairmen wrote to Pope John Paul II and Archbishop Runcie with the suggestion that a new commission be appointed, and with two questions pertaining to the *Final Report*:

> Are these Agreed Statements and their Elucidations consonant in substance with the faith of the Catholic Church and the Anglican Communion?

> Does the *Final Report* offer a sufficient basis for taking the next step towards reconciliation?

While a number of local churches and individuals offered their opinions, two different processes were set in place by the authorities of the Catholic Church and the Anglican Communion. The Pope asked the CDF to make a doctrinal examination of the Report, its first response being *The Observations*[269] of March 1982. In a letter to the Catholic co-chairman of ARCIC, Cardinal Ratzinger spoke of the Report as a significant step in the reconciliation of the two communions, though it was not an 'agreement which is truly substantial'.[270] The Report comments especially on doctrinal issues requiring further study and clarification. Only at this point was the *Final Report*, with *The Observations* of the CDF, released to the Catholic episcopal conferences around the world.

The Anglican approach was to send the *Final Report* to the 29 provinces, a reflection on the autonomy of the provinces.

---

269 'The *Observations* of the Congregation for the Doctrine of the Faith on the Final Report of ARCIC I (1982)' in *Anglicans and Roman Catholics: The Search for Unity*, London: SPCK/CTS, 1994: 79–91.

270 'Letter by Cardinal J. Ratzinger (Prefect of the Congregation for the Doctrine of the Faith) to Bishop Alan Clark (Roman Catholic Co-Chairman of ARCIC I) (1982)' in *Anglicans and Roman Catholics*: 92.

Their responses were collated in *The Emmaus Report*[271] in preparation for the Lambeth Conference of 1988, which would express the mind of the Communion. The bishops at Lambeth judged that the Agreed Statements and their Elucidations are 'consonant in substance with the faith of Anglicans and believes that this agreement offers a sufficient basis for taking the next step towards the reconciliation of our two Churches'.[272] The Conference recognized consensus and convergence among the Provinces of the Communion and gave a positive response on Eucharist, Ministry and Ordination, though it asked for further study on several authority issues. Some responses were in the manner of a testing of the *Final Report* against the sixteenth-century formularies, particularly the Thirty-Nine Articles. As Bishop John Hind points out, this approach was not in line with the method of ARCIC which sought to get behind past controversial expressions.[273]

It was unfortunate that the official Catholic response to ARCIC was not on the table at Lambeth. It was eventually published under the auspices of PCPCU and the CDF. Despite this double patronage the *Final Response* showed a significant resemblance to the 1982 *Observations* and very few traces of the English and French-speaking episcopal conferences whose input PCPCU had sought.

The Catholic response was finally published in 1991. It spoke of matters essential to Catholic doctrine, for example, certain authority issues, which would require deep study. Then, there are other matters where progress was evident – Eucharist, Ministry and Ordination – though clarifications would be necessary. The CDF's methodology is widely regarded as one that requires Anglican conformity with Catholic expressions of faith, and thus 'implicitly disapproves of the ARCIC method'.[274]

---

271 *The Emmaus Report*, London: Church House Publishing, 1987.
272 'The 1988 Lambeth Conference: Resolution 8 and Explanatory Note regarding ARCIC I' in *Anglicans and Roman Catholics*: 153.
273 John Hind, 'What We Agree in Faith in the Light of the ARCIC *Final Report*?' in *One in Christ* January 2004: 35.
274 Hind: 37.

Many commentators have been severely critical of the CDF's approach. Among them is Francis J. Sullivan who accepts that an agreed ecumenical statement should be consonant with the faith of the Catholic Church, but he questions any requirement that, in order to avoid ambiguity, it must be expressed in the precise formulas used by the Catholic Church.[275] Henry Chadwick remarked that the Commission was heartened when it heard John Paul II's words of approval in 1980, affirming their method of 'going behind habits of thought and expression born and nourished in enmity and controversy'.[276] Chadwick identifies a point of difference, that whereas for Anglicans the truth of a definition 'primarily hangs on the content being consonant with Scripture and accepted sacred tradition, and therefore more on the content than on the organs of authority', for Catholics 'the truth of a definition depends less on the *content* and more on the primate or the general council *by whom* the definition is given'.[277]

In May 1982, during John Paul II's visit to England, he and Archbishop Runcie signed a *Common Declaration*, reflecting on the work of ARCIC and announcing that there would be a new Commission. Thus, all that we have so far considered comes under the title of ARCIC I.

ARCIC II

The co-chairmen of ARCIC II during its first years, Anglican Bishop Mark Santer and Catholic Bishop Cormac Murphy-O'Connor, made the point that the primary task of the new commission was to examine and try to resolve the remaining divisive matters of doctrine. The enlarged membership of 27 people, who were more internationally representative than was

---

275 Francis J. Sullivan, 'The Vatican Response to Vatican I (1992)' in *Anglicans and Roman Catholics*: 298–308.
276 Henry Chadwick, 'Blocked approaches'. *The Tablet* 1 February 1992: 136.
277 Ibid: 137.

the situation at ARCIC I, included two women. The expanded membership made debate more difficult.

The Anglican Consultative Council suggested to the commission that it first address 'justification' in order to assure evangelical Anglicans that the two communions believe in justification by faith through grace.

Salvation and the Church: 1987

In the preface to this first Agreed Statement of the new commission, the co-chairmen explain that to properly discuss the doctrine of justification it must be considered in the wider context of the doctrine of salvation. Hence the title, *Salvation and the Church*. The report lists four difficulties which the commission explores: the understanding of the faith through which we are justified, the meaning of justification, the place of good works in relation to salvation and the role of the Church in the process of salvation. Over the centuries, it was acknowledged, each side developed caricatures of the other's beliefs, which were not at all helpful. As a result of the work of this commission and the help received from the prior Lutheran–Roman Catholic Consultation in the United States, the report states that 'our two Communions are agreed on the essential aspects of the doctrine of salvation and on the Church's role within it'.[278] In other words, as far as salvation and the Church are concerned, there are no lingering reasons to justify the two communions remaining separated.

Two years later, in 1988, 'the judgement of the Congregation for the Doctrine of the Faith on this report is . . . substantially positive', though it was unable 'to affirm that ARCIC II had arrived at substantial agreement'.[279] The CDF requested a more

---

278 *Salvation and the Church: An Agreed Statement by the Second Anglican–Roman Catholic International Commission. ARCIC II*, London: Church House Publishing, 1987: n 32.
279 Congregation for the Doctrine of the Faith, *Observations on Salvation and the Church of ARCIC II*, London: Catholic Truth Society, 1988: 3–5.

profound study of a number of issues, particularly related to the doctrine of the Church.

Church as Communion: 1991

The CDF's *Observations on Salvation and the Church* prompted ARCIC II to write a further document on the Church, partly as a way of responding to the revisions requested and partly as a way of moving the dialogue in a more positive direction. Whereas the previous documents sought to reach agreements on doctrines which hitherto were points of division, *Church as Communion* highlights the 'real though as yet imperfect' communion of the two communions. This short, though important, document offers an ecclesial framework for the whole of ARCIC's work. In a few paragraphs it sketches a portrait of the Church in which we – Catholics and Anglicans – are to be together.

Koinonia, which translates as 'communion' or 'fellowship', is in the first place the life of the persons of the Trinity into which all the baptized are drawn. This inner, invisible life has a visible expression: the one apostolic faith of the baptized, the one celebration of the Eucharist, a single ministry of oversight and a shared commitment to the mission given the Church by Christ.

After identifying the elements of communion already existing between Anglicans and Catholics, the Commission named three unresolved matters that should be addressed in subsequent dialogues: the reconciliation of the ordained ministries, the ways in which each Church arrives at its moral teaching, and the question of authority in the Church. Though the statement is not an authoritative declaration by either Church, publication was permitted in order to promote discussion on it. One official contributor to the discussion, without making reference by name to the report, was a CDF 'Letter to the Bishops of the Catholic Church on Some Aspects of the Church Understood as Communion',[280] dated 28 May 1992.

---

280 *Origins*, 25 June 1992: 108–12.

Clarifications on aspects of the Agreed Statements on Eucharist and Ministry of ARCIC I: 1993

In the 1991 response by the Catholic Church to the *Final Report* the request was made for clarification on four points about the Eucharist and another four on Ordination and Ministry. A sub-committee of ARCIC II worked on the questions, and the clarifications they made were submitted to the Catholic authorities in 1993. PCPCU responded, saying, 'The agreement reached on Eucharist and Ministry by ARCIC I is thus greatly strengthened and no further study would seem to be required at this stage.' The letter concluded with a further affirmation, that 'the remarkable consensus reached up to now on the themes dealt with by ARCIC I will only be able to be seen in its full light and importance as the work of ARCIC II proceeds'.[281]

Life in Christ: Morals, Communion and the Church: 1994

Life in Christ: Morals, Communion and the Church is the first bilateral dialogue on moral issues. In their introduction to this report, the co-chairmen wrote that 'the Gospel we proclaim cannot be divorced from the life we live'. Whereas all the previous ARCIC reports were on doctrinal matters, the time had arrived for the commission to study the moral teachings of both churches and to assess the existing level of communion on morality. One reason for embarking on this first-ever international dialogue on morals, was because of a widespread perception – or misperception – that the two communions are 'divided most sharply by their moral teaching'.[282] The commission made

---

281 Letter of Edward Cardinal Cassidy to the Co-Chairmen of ARCIC-II, 11 March 1994, in *Clarifications of certain aspects of the Agreed Statements on Eucharist and Ministry of the first Anglican-Roman Catholic International Commission*. London: The Anglican Consultative Council and The Pontifical Council for Promoting Christian Unity, 1994: 12–13.
282 *Church as Communion. An Agreed Statement by the Second Anglican–Roman Catholic International Commission. ARCIC II.* London: Church House Publishing, 1991: 1.

two discoveries: the first, that many of the preconceptions about each other's moral teaching were little more than caricatures, and the second, that the differences which do exist take on a new complexion when they are seen in their origin and context.[283]

There are two moral issues on which the two Communions have expressed official disagreement, and which the commission studied, namely remarriage after divorce and contraception. There are other areas of disagreement, though not officially pronounced on, which are mentioned in the report, without any detailed discussion. The overall conclusion is that whereas the two communions have historically developed their moral teachings in isolation from one another, and the differences between them are serious, 'careful study and consideration has shown they are not fundamental'.[284] As with all ARCIC statements, the text was published in order to promote discussion on the subject and is not an authoritative declaration of either Church.

The Gift of Authority: Authority in the Church III: 1999

The first Statement on Authority in the Church was published in 1976, followed by an Elucidation and a second Statement in 1981. The official responses by the Lambeth Conference in 1988 on behalf of the Anglican Communion, and by the Catholic Church in 1991, recommended continued study of authority issues. A long time in the making, and building on the foundations set in place by the previous documents, this new statement offers a further and significant development in understanding authority as 'a gift that God intends for all Christian Churches',[285] which they are to make their own.

---

283 *Life in Christ. Morals, Communion and the Church. An Agreed Statement by the Second Anglican–Roman Catholic Commission. ARCIC II.* London: Church House Publishing and Catholic Truth Society, 1994: n 50.
284 Ibid: n 88.
285 John Baycroft, 'Challenges of *The Gift of Authority* for the Churches', *Bulletin/Centro Pro Unione*: 58, 2000: 18.

'Authority' is thus placed in the realm of grace. Bishop John Baycroft's advice is that this closely argued text in which every sentence depends on the previous one, ought to be approached as a pilgrimage from the beginning. It challenges the Churches to understand authority as a gift from the author of life, and therefore is of its nature life-giving and gracious. If one can get into this mode of thinking then it becomes hard to say 'No' to God when he offers this gift.[286]

The revelation of God in the scriptures is transmitted to succeeding generations of Christians enabling them to hear the 'yes' of Jesus to God, and to add their 'amen' to it. Within this tradition, bishops are entrusted with a ministry of memory so that 'not only from generation to generation, but also from place to place, the one faith is communicated and lived out . . . Thus the *sensus fidelium* of the people of God and the ministry of memory exist together in reciprocal relationship.'[287] The Agreement then speaks of the exercise of authority in the Church through synodality and communion, and the maintenance of the Church in truth through teaching and conciliar, collegial and primatial forms of government.

Both Churches are equally challenged by the *Gift*, because neither have got it right. Anglicans are looking for structures of coherence, including a development of the role of the Archbishop of Canterbury having pastoral oversight of the provinces of the Communion. But the very suggestion of somehow or other forfeiting absolute provincial autonomy might trigger more disintegration within the Communion, unless together the provinces can name those key moments when they must do things together. The Catholic Church, having developed a kind of synodical government since Vatican II, has in practice, not governed synodically, but by way of a centralized system which

---

286 Notes taken from talk given by Bishop Baycroft, *Centro pro Unione* 21 October 1999.
287 *The Gift of Authority. Authority in the Church III. An Agreed Statement by the Anglican Roman Catholic International Commission. ARCIC II*, London and New York: Catholic Truth Society and Church Publishing Incorporated, 1999: n 30.

some would describe as oppressive. For Catholics it is a matter of bringing Vatican I and II together, the two supreme authorities of the Bishop of Rome and the College of Bishops.

The statement lists eleven advances in agreement, and a number of issues facing both communions. Two significant points conclude the Commission's work: one is an appeal to both communions to make more visible now the *koinonia* they already enjoy, and the second is a proposal that Anglicans and Catholics 're-receive' the universal primacy of the bishop of Rome. Bishop Baycroft comments on this proposal that, if the Petrine ministry is a gift of God to the Church, then the Catholic Church cannot continue to hold it in such a way that others cannot receive it. Herein lies a challenge to Catholics and Anglicans to respond to n 95 and n 96 of *Ut Unum Sint* where John Paul II speaks of exercising the primacy 'in a way that is open to a new situation'. To this end he invites 'Church leaders and their theologians' to become active in the dialogue. Important in the process will be the part played by the Vatican itself.[288] Though John Paul's pontificate ended on 2 April 2005, the Catholic Church's commitment to ecumenism remains firmly in place, which must include a shared dialogue over the primacy.

Mary: Grace and Hope in Christ: 2005

For almost five years ARCIC II worked on the role of Mary in the life and doctrine of the Church, the end-product being *Mary: Grace and Hope in Christ.* The subtitle, *Hope in Christ,* indicates the direction of the Agreed Statement, that it is not solely reflective in style, but very much an eschatological statement. Yes, it is an agreed statement, but at the same time it is a troubling document to some in the evangelical wing of the Anglican Communion and to those Reformation Christians who are wedded only to a literal interpretation of the Bible. The text accepts that a range of readings of scripture is not only per-

---

288 John Paul II, *Ut Unum Sint,* Vatican City: Libreria Editrice Vaticana, 1995.

missible but well understood in contemporary scholarly circles (paragraph 7).

The Gift of Authority, 1981, is a prerequisite to this Mary document because it indicates the level of agreement already achieved, and it nominates the areas still requiring study. Reception and re-reception, as understood in *The Gift*, enables Christian people who may have forgotten, neglected or even abused aspects of the apostolic tradition, to re-enter scripture and tradition in order to recapture the fullness of their heritage. This particular exercise by Anglican and Catholic scholars aims at re-receiving together the story and meaning of Mary's place in God's revelation.

There are 80 paragraphs: an Introduction and five subject areas. The first section: 'Mary according to the Scriptures', unfolds not according to any critical methodology addressing disputed questions but by allowing the scriptures to contribute to the making of theology. In fact, paragraph 6 says: 'Indeed, it is impossible to be faithful to Scripture and not to take Mary seriously.' For centuries Anglicans and Catholics viewed the scriptures through different lenses; here they research together about Mary in the context of the whole of the New Testament, in the context of the Old Testament and in the light of tradition. Christians understand that 'the birth of Mary's son is the fulfilment of God's plan for Israel, and Mary's part in that fulfilment is that of free and unqualified consent . . . "Behold I am the handmaid of the Lord; let it be done to me according to your word"' (paragraph 11). The scriptural section unfolds over 24 paragraphs and the last one states that 'The scriptural witness summons all believers in every generation to call Mary "blessed"' (paragraph 30).

The second section, 'Mary in the Christian Tradition', is a sweep across history beginning from the first centuries of the Christian era, through the Middle Ages to the Reformation and the present day. It was in the late Middle Ages when theology was less rooted in scripture and spirituality was straying from theology, that the Reformers reacted to the Marian excesses, thus establishing a large Christian stream in which Mary was little noticed. As time passed, positions hardened so that Catholics were identified by their emphasis on devotion to Mary, and other Western Christians by an absence of any notable attention to her.

The third section, 'Mary Within the Pattern of Grace and Hope', relying on Romans 8.30, speaks of her as 'marked out from the beginning as the one chosen, called and graced by God through the Holy Spirit for the task that lay ahead of her' (paragraph 54). She accepted God's will, and thus became the faithful disciple who is also 'a sign of hope for all humanity' (paragraph 56). It is in this context that the two papal definitions of the Immaculate Conception (1854) and the Assumption (1950) are considered. Charles Sherlock, a member of the commission, speaks of a prior theological method which saw human beings as created and sinful; a contemporary approach places stress more on what human beings will become. The starting point, in line with Paul's thinking, is the ascended Christ and the vision of a new humanity. Mary fits this pattern, hence the title of the document: *Mary: Grace and Hope in Christ,* and the readiness to acknowledge that the two dogmas 'understood within the biblical pattern of the economy of grace and hope outlined here, can be said to be consonant with the teaching of the Scriptures and the ancient common traditions' (paragraph 60).

The fourth section, 'Mary in the life of the Church', makes a useful point that various traditions have had their own individual styles of appropriating Mary's way of living out the grace of God. For instance, Anglicans might begin with reflection on the scriptural example of Mary, whereas Catholics have tended to emphasize Mary's ministry on our behalf (paragraph 65). The twentieth century is witness to a growing convergence of the thinking of the two traditions. Other subjects considered include the practice of seeking Mary's intercession, the distinctive ministry of Mary given her relationship to Jesus, devotions in honour of her and apparitions.

The Conclusion serves as both a summary and a means of highlighting important points. There is a reaffirmation of the relevant material in *Authority in the Church*. The document confirms that a 'growing convergence' allowed the commission to approach questions about Mary in a fresh way, that is, in the pattern of grace and hope. They conclude with five points of agreement and with the assertion that what they have discovered favours further reconciliation by the two Churches.

A helpful addition to *Mary: Grace and Hope in Christ* are two commentaries, one by Jared Wicks, the other by Timothy Bradshaw. Both examine the four sections of the document, going beyond summaries with useful critiques. Wicks draws attention to the uniqueness of its biblical interpretation, which is done in the light of tradition. He reflects further on Mary as 'the fullest human example of the life of grace' and the implications for Christians today. Bradshaw observes that 'ARCIC has been honest in producing a document in basically a Roman Catholic mode so that Anglicans can get the feel of what is being needed by Roman Catholics in any reunited Church'. A very useful addition is a study guide, in the form of questions, which he provides after his reflections on each section.

Thus, the work of ARCIC II reached its end in 2005. Current suggestions include that the Agreed Statements be published in one volume, and that a process for their reception be set in place. Though no request has been made of the two communions for an official response to ARCIC II along the lines of the one given to the *Final Report* of ARCIC I, it is even uncertain if such a request will be made. There are other possible ways of effecting reception within the communions. An obvious way is that employed at Mississauga, a style that could be adapted for use among a variety of people, bishops, clergy and laity.

The agenda for the third phase of ARCIC is expected to be announced towards the end of 2006.

Beginnings of the International Anglican Roman Catholic Commission for Unity and Mission (IARCCUM)

The Common Declaration: 1996

The beginnings of IARCCUM can be traced to the 1996 joint statement of John Paul II and Archbishop Carey. Their *Common Declaration* said:

> The obstacle to reconciliation caused by the ordination of women as priests and bishops in some provinces of the Anglican Communion has also become increasingly evident, creating a new situation. In view of this, it may be opportune at this stage in our journey to consult further about how the relationship between the Anglican Communion and the Catholic Church is to progress.[289]

Neither leader could find a way forward, but this did not mean a downgrading of relations. They chose instead to call for two things: further consultation so as to find a way forward, and a programme of reception of the texts of ARCIC II.

The Mississauga Meeting: 2000

Given the 'agenda' suggested in the *Common Declaration*, Archbishop Carey and Cardinal Cassidy proceeded to convene a six-day meeting of Anglican and Catholic bishops in May of 2000 in Mississauga, Canada. The bishops came in pairs from 13 countries to carry out two principal tasks: (1) to review together the state of Anglican–Catholic relations on the ground and to consider advances made by the Anglican–Roman Catholic International Commission; (2) to consider what the next step in Anglican–Catholic relations should be, given current experience and theological advances.[290] Only one major paper was

---

289 'The Common Declaration' of 5 December 1996, in *Information Service* 94, 1997/1: 20–1.
290 Mary Tanner, 'A Unique Meeting in Mississauga' in *One in Christ* January 2004: 3–6.

presented, and that was by Father Jean-Marie Tillard, entitled 'Our goal: full Visible Communion'; otherwise the meeting was very much a working session for the bishops.

Whereas the work of ARCIC was principally that of theologians, now it was placed in the hands of bishops, the pastoral leaders of the churches. They spoke of their local situations and reviewed the work of ARCIC, discussing what might be the next step between the two Communions. Their report, *Communion in Mission* recommended:

(1) Preparation of a Joint Declaration of Agreement which would formally express the degree of agreement that already exists between the two Communions.
(2) Guide and promote the study and reception of the Agreed Statements.
(3) Search for strategies to translate the degree of spiritual communion achieved into visible and practical outcomes.

The International Anglican Roman Catholic Commission for Unity and Mission (IARCCUM)

The two Communions wasted little time in setting up the recommended new Commission. The first meeting of IARCCUM was held in London and Rome, 20–24 November 2001, under the co-chairmanship of Catholic Archbishop John Bathersby of Brisbane and Anglican Bishop David Beetge of South Africa. In London, Archbishop Carey said he saw its work as putting 'into practice the mutual commitment and common life that is already ours'. And, in Rome, Pope John Paul II said the body was in place to consolidate the gains already made, and to lead us to new depths of communion.

Work has begun on a common declaration which would seek to name the areas of agreement in faith that exist between Anglicans and Catholics, and acknowledging the differences that still need to be addressed. As far as the reception of the ARCIC Agreed Statements is concerned, it is worth remembering the model that had been set in place at Mississauga, which is easily transferable to any part of the world for use by any group. Many of the bishops who gathered there began with a very thin knowledge of *ARCIC*, but they enjoyed a lived experience of ARCIC for the days they were together and left better informed and committed to the cause of the full visible communion of the two churches.

The enthusiastic beginnings, and short life of IARCCUM, was dealt something of a blow by the decision of ECUSA to ordain an actively gay man as bishop of New Hampshire. A press release of December 2003 reported a meeting of Cardinal Walter Kasper of PCPCU and Canon John Peterson, Secretary General of the Anglican Consultative Council, when ' . . . the future of Anglican Roman Catholic dialogue was discussed, especially in the light of recent developments within the life of the Anglican Communion'.[291] The outcome was that the planned work of IARCCUM, the publication and reception of a Common Statement of Faith, would be 'put on hold in the light of ecclesiological concerns raised as a consequence of these events'. The point was also made that suspending the meeting did not mean an end of the dialogue.

In fact, it was decided that after the publication of *Mary: Grace and Hope in Christ* on 16 May 2005, IARCCUM will resume its review of the work of ARCIC II. They will synthesize ARCIC II and offer it to the Anglican and Catholic authorities as a step in the process of reception. Special attention will be given to fostering the reception of the Mary document.

---

291 'Statement on the International Anglican Roman Catholic Commission for Unity and Mission (IARCCUM)' www.catholic-ew.org. uk/CN/03/031204.htm

Selected Bibliography

Alberigo, Giuseppe, ed., *A History of Vatican II*. Komonchak, Joseph (English editor). Volume I (1995), Volume II (1997), Volume III (2000), Volume IV (2002). Leuven and Maryknoll: Peeters and Orbis.

Barlow, Bernard OSM, *The Malines Conversations 1921–1925*. Norwich: The Canterbury Press, 1996.

Bea, Augustin Cardinal, *Unity in Freedom: Reflections on the Human Family*. New York: Harper and Row, 1964.

Bea, Augustin Cardinal, *The Way to Unity after the Council*. London: Geoffrey Chapman, 1967.

Bill, E. G. W. *Anglican Initiatives in Christian Unity: Lectures Delivered in Lambeth Palace Library 1966*. London: SPCK, 1967.

Carpenter, Humphrey, *Robert Runcie: The Reluctant Archbishop*. London: Hodder and Stoughton, 1996.

Chadwick, Owen, *The Reformation*. Rev. edn. Harmondsworth: Penguin Books, 1972.

Chadwick, Owen, *Britain and the Vatican during the Second World War*. Cambridge: Cambridge University Press, 1986.

Chadwick, Owen, *Michael Ramsey: A Life*. Oxford: Clarendon Press, 1990.

Clark, Kenneth, *Civilisation*. London: BBC, 1969.

Duggan, Margaret, *Runcie: The Making of an Archbishop*. London: Hodder and Stoughton, 1983.

Findlow, Irina, *Journey into Unity*. London: New City, 1975.

Hastings, Adrian, *A History of English Christianity 1920–1985*. London: Collins, 1986.

Hebblethwaite, Peter, *In the Vatican*. Bethesda: Adler and Adler, 1986.

Hebblethwaite, Peter, *Paul VI: The First Modern Pope*. London: HarperCollins, 1993.

Hill, Christopher, 'Friendship Before Theology in Runcie and the Churches' in *Runcie on Reflection*, Stephen Platten, ed., Norwich: Canterbury Press, 2003.

Hill, Christopher and Yarnold, Edward SJ, Eds., *Anglicans and Roman Catholics: The Search for Unity*. London: SPCK/CTS, 1994.

Selected Bibliography

Jasper, Ronald C. D. *George Bell: Bishop of Chichester*. London: Oxford University Press, 1967.

Koet, Josepha et al., *Hearth of Unity: Forty Years of Foyer Unitas 1952–1992*. Bethany: Fratelli Palombi Editori, 1996.

Lambeth Commission on Communion. *The Windsor Report 2004*. London: The Anglican Communion Office, 2004.

Longley, Clifford, *The Worlock Archive*. London and New York: Geoffrey Chapman, 2000.

Lowrie, Walter, *Fifty Years of St Paul's American Church*. Rome 1926.

Manktelow, Michael, *John Moorman*. Norwich: Canterbury Press, 1999.

Millon, Judith Rice, *St. Paul's Within-the-Walls, Rome*. Roma: Edizioni Dell'Elefante, 2001.

Moorman, John, *Vatican Observed: An Anglican Impression of Vatican II*. London: Darton, Longman and Todd, 1967.

Nevin R. J., *St Paul's Within the Walls: An Account of the American Chapel at Rome, Italy*. New York: Appleton, 1878.

Pawley, Bernard, *Looking at the Vatican Council*. London: SCM Press, 1962.

Pawley, Bernard and Margaret, *Rome and Canterbury Through Four Centuries*. London: Mowbrays, 1974.

Pawley, Bernard, ed., *The Second Vatican Council: Studies by Eight Anglican Observers*. London: Oxford University Press, 1967.

Pawley, Margaret, *Donald C. Servant of Christ*. London: SPCK, 1987.

Platten, Stephen, *Augustine's Legacy: Authority and Leadership in the Anglican Communion*. London: Darton Longman and Todd, 1997.

Platten, Stephen, ed., *Anglicanism and the Western Christian Tradition*. Norwich: Canterbury Press, 2003.

Podmore, Colin, *Aspects of Anglican Identity*. London: Church House Publishing, 2005.

Purdy, William, *The Search for Unity: Relations Between the Anglican and Roman Catholic Churches From the 1950's to the 1970's*. London: Geoffrey Chapman, 1996.

Rynne, Xavier, *Vatican Council II*. New York: Orbis, 1999.

Slack, George, *George Bell*. London: SCM Press, 1971.

Smith, Patrick, *A Desk in Rome*. London: Collins, 1974.

Stacpoole, Alberic, ed., *Vatican II, by those who were there*. London: Geoffrey Chapman, 1986.

Strudwick, Vincent, *Towards an Anglican Understanding of the Church*. London: Darton, Longman and Todd, 1994.

Sykes, Norman, *William Wake, Archbishop of Canterbury 1657–1737*. Vol. I. London: Cambridge University Press, 1957.

Villain, Maurice, *Unity: A History and Some Reflections*. London: Harvill Press, 1963. [English translation of *Introduction a' l'Oecuménisme*, Tournai: Casterman, 1961]

Index

Index

Index

Index

Haering, Bernard 55
Hall, Miss 21
Halliburton, John 93
Hammett, Barry 104
Hastings, Adrian 30, 51, 53, 54
Heath, Mark 19, 111
Hebblethwaite, Peter 44, 54, 140
Heenan, Cardinal John 53-7, 70, 84, 97
Heim, Archbishop Bruno 101
Helmsing, Bishop Charles 150
Henry VII 17
Henry VIII 2, 15, 17
Herriman, William 22
Hickling, Colin 36-7
Hill, Christopher 112, 116-17, 152, 154
Hill, Edmund 152
Hind, Bishop John 161
Hines, Bishop John 99
Hinsley, Cardinal Arthur 30
Holy Office 69-70
Hooker, Richard 4
Hope, Archbishop David 132
Howard, Henry 18
Howe, Bishop John 100, 106
Hue, Corbet 20
Humanae Salutis 60
Humani Generis 42
Hume, Cardinal Basil 116

IARCCUM xviii, 9, 134, 138, 149, 150, 172, 173, 174

Ida, Signora 102
Immaculate Conception 88, 170
Indulgences 75
Infallibility 21, 71, 120, 139, 151, 157, 159
Instruments of Unity 6, 10, 11, 12
Ius divinum 158

Jackson, Dr Joseph 62
James I. 15
James, Bishop Colin 36
Jefferson, Ingleby 114
Jewel, John 5
Joel Nafuma Refugee Center 24
John XXIII 17, 25, 28, 38, 39, 41, 47, 58, 60-1, 65, 67, 69
John Paul II 17, 19, 89, 100, 103, 116, 118, 125-7, 130, 136-7, 140, 154, 156, 160, 162, 168, 172-3
Johnstone, Virginia xviii, 23, 49, 82-3, 96, 121
Jones, Leander 16
Jurisdiction 13-14, 139, 157, 159
Justification 3, 43, 126, 163

Kasper, Cardinal Walter 9, 134, 138, 143, 147-8, 174
Kelly, Herbert 118
Kelly, J.N.D. 43
Kemp, Bishop Eric 113

181

Index

Index